6.67

ABSOLUTELY ESSENTIAL UTILITIES FOR THE IBM PC

Emily Rosenthal

MIS: *PRESS*

MANAGEMENT INFORMATION SOURCE, INC.

COPYRIGHT

TRADEMARKS

PC DOS and IBM PC are trademarks of IBM Corporation
Okidata is a trademark of Okidata Corporation
MS DOS is a trademark of Microsoft Corporation
dBASE II, III, III PLUS, and MultiMate are trademarks of Ashton-Tate
Wordstar Professional 3.3 and Release 4 are trademarks of MicroPro
Lotus 1-2-3 and Symphony are trademarks of Lotus Development Corp
Macintosh is a trademark of Apple Corporation
Dfixer is a trademark of MicroWay
Disk Optimizer is a trademark of SoftLogic Solutions, Inc.
DSRECOVER is a trademark of Design Software, Inc.
Mace + is a trademark of Paul Mace Software
Norton Utilities and Norton Commander are trademarks of Peter Norton Computing, Inc.
1dir + and WordPlus are trademarks of Bourbaki, Inc.
XTREE is a trademark of Executive Systems, Inc.
PC Tools is a trademark of Central Point Software, Inc.
File Facility is a trademark of IBM
Filepath is a trademark of SDA Associates
Smartpath is a trademark of Software Research Technologies
DOS Commander is a trademark of Connecticut Software Systems Corporation
EASY-DOS-IT is a trademark of BMS Computer, Inc.
Direct Access is a trademark of Delta Technology International, Inc.
Microsoft Windows is a trademark of Microsoft Corporation
Taskview is a trademark of Sunny Hill Software
DESQview is a trademark of Quarterdeck Office Systems
Memory/Shift is a trademark of North American Business Systems, Inc.
DoubleDOS is a trademark of SoftLogic Solutions, Inc.
ProKey is a trademark of RoseSoft, Inc.
SmartKey is a trademark of Software Research Technologies, Inc.
Keyworks is a trademark of Alpha Software Corporation
The Spreadsheet Auditor is a trademark of Computer Associates International, Inc.
Cell/Mate is a trademark of Clarity Software Corporation
SOS is a trademark of Goldata Computer Services, Inc.
Note-It is a trademark of Turner Hall Publishing
PC Converter Plus and Reports Plus are trademarks of Softsync, Inc.
Quicksilver is a trademark of WordTech Systems, Inc.
Quickcode Plus and Quickreport are trademarks of Fox & Geller, Inc.
Clipper is a trademark of Nantucket, Inc.
FoxBase + is a trademark of Fox Software
Flashcode is a trademark of The Software Bottling Co.
R&R is a trademark of Concentric Data Systems, Inc.
SBT Database Accounting Library is a trademark of SBT Corp.
Disk Technician is a trademark of Prime Solutions, Inc.
Disk Explorer is a trademark of Quaid Software Limited
Utilities I and Utilities II are trademarks of IBM
DISK P.M. is a trademark of Digital Pathways, Inc.
DiskMate and G-Direct are trademarks of Pico Publishing
Diskette Manager II is a trademark of Lassen Software, Inc.
DOS Helper is a trademark of MetaWare, Inc.
DOS File Tracker and File Command II are trademarks of IBM
File Mate is a trademark of Intersecting Concepts
PathMinder is a trademark of Westlake Data Corp.
DPATH-PLUS is a trademark of Personal Business Solutions, Inc.
Program Manager is a trademark of Lessen Software, Inc.
DOSEASE is a trademark of Software Solutions, Inc.
DOS-HELPER is a trademark of Aristo Software
Task Director is a trademark of IBM Corp.
Top View is a trademark of IBM Corp.

TABLE OF CONTENTS

INTRODUCTION

Utilities are support programs that protect and extend the potential of your hardware and application software programs. With the exception of the chapters on application-specific utilities, most of the utilities covered in this book can enhance your operations across all of your applications.

Utilities address your ancillary needs rather than your primary computing purposes. As such, they tend to be smaller programs in terms of bytes and lower in price than the primary application programs they support, such as word processors, spreadsheet software, and data base managers.

The discussions in this book are aimed at computer users whose systems have mid-level hardware configurations. Although many of these utilities can take full advantage of a variety of enhancements, all of their features are available with a single-user IBM PC, XT, or AT compatible with 512K RAM, a monochrome monitor with a graphics adaptor board, and a floppy diskette drive and hard disk drive. Most of the utilities are equally compatible with the same system minus the hard disk and graphics board.

The Problem

Necessity is the mother of utilities. Computers and software applications were originally invented together. Now, new applications are designed when programmers realize the potential of their computing power. New hardware is then designed to realize more from those applications.

No outside force is coordinating this proliferation of hardware peripherals and application programs. Neither the introduction of new products nor the technological improvements are following any overall plan. The resulting growth, then, is both beneficial and problematic.

While there are many products to choose from, they vary greatly. The strengths in one show the weaknesses in others, and the differences between them affect their ability to work with each other.

Some obstacles that arise are eventually resolved by hardware or operating system enhancements or by the adoption of advanced standards by application developers. Utilities are designed to address the difficult issues that occur before more general solutions are universally put in place.

More often than not, an inventive user figures out a solution to work around his or her own specific predicament. If the solution appears to have general "utility," it is packaged and marketed.

The areas that computer users have found problematic are also the subjects of utility programs:

- hardware limitations
- software limitations
- managing several applications
- software/hardware incompatibility

This book addresses those problems and discusses utilities designed to solve them.

Hardware Limitations

Your computer's hardware can inhibit your computing efficiency. Inherent limits in hardware capacity and capabilities may stop you long before your software's capabilities and your creativity run out. Your computing also may be obstructed by hardware malfunctions wherein your computer performs at less-than-full potential.

Ironically perhaps, hardware limitations can often be alleviated by software. The software solutions are frequently less expensive than replacing or purchasing additional hardware; moreover, software solutions may exist where hardware solutions are not yet available at any price.

Chapter 1, "Disk Maintenance Utilities," addresses the issue of hardware failure and inefficiency, particularly as it affects hard disks.

Chapter 5, "Multi-Tasking Utilities," addresses the issue of managing RAM, which in the past was solely controlled by the hardware.

Chapter 10, "Communications Utilities," provides some inexpensive methods that enable computers to work together.

Chapter 12, "Backup Utilities," provides mechanisms by which you can cope with hardware failures.

Software Limitations

Obstructions due to software limitations appear at two levels:

- operating system software
- application software

The **operating system** provides the general mechanisms through which both the user and the application software interact with the computer. If the operating system provided every useful capability, and every application took advantage of every capability, there would be no problems; however, this situation is not the case.

At one extreme, some application software packages bypass the operating system to accomplish tasks that the operating system cannot handle. At the other extreme, some application software packages have not kept pace with enhancements to the operating system's capabilities.

Chapter 2 "File Management Utilities," addresses the difficulties of performing such tasks using DOS facilities alone.

Chapter 3, "Path Utilities," addresses the limitations of subdirectory access by DOS as well as the inability of some applications to take advantage of the facilities DOS does offer.

Chapter 6, "Keyboard Macro Utilities," extends the capabilities of application software as well as DOS.

Chapters 7 and 8 cover spreadsheet and data base utilities and address users who are happy with the general operation of their choice of application software but want additional features.

Chapter 11, "Developers' Tools," provides debugging assistance, shortcuts, and extended capabilities for programmers.

Managing Several Applications

The sheer number of applications for which the computer is now regularly used adds an element of disorder. Though most users maintain only one version of a specific application, it is very common for more than one application to be used on the same computer.

The dilemmas that normally arise as a result of using several applications include the following:

- accessing applications
- using applications together

This multi-purpose use of the computer requires a fair amount of thoughtful organization of program and data files. Furthermore, if more than one user needs access to one or more applications, the different users' needs must be considered.

Chapter 2, "File Management Utilities," addresses the process of organizing applications and maintaining that organization.

Chapter 3, "Path Utilities," and Chapter 4, "DOS Menu Utilities," address the problem of accessing applications and data files once they have been organized.

Chapter 5, "Multi-Tasking Utilities," addresses the issue of using several applications together.

Software/Hardware Incompatibility

Software is written with hardware in mind. You may purchase new hardware products with new features, but your software may have no facility for taking advantage of those features.

Nowhere is this problem more apparent than between application software and printers. There are hundreds of different printers available, each with unique capabilities accessed by different software controls.

Many application developers periodically update their software to take advantage of new hardware; however, there is often a time lag, the updates may be costly, and/or the updates may not address your particular needs.

Chapter 9, "Printer Utilities," addresses how to take advantage of your printer's potential when your application software does not.

Utilities Strategy

Do it your way: when choosing and using utilities, always remember that your goal is to simplify your life, not over-complicate it. The best way to approach any utility is to use it to solve problems you already know you have. Always keep in mind the reason the utility interested you in the first place.

Wait until after you have solved your immediate problems and until time and experience have proved software and hardware compatibility. Only then should you experiment with those features that solve problems you didn't know you had.

Consider other users also. If you are choosing and setting up utilities to use yourself, your considerations will be very different than if you are an expert setting up a system for nontechnical users.

Program File Management

The very nature of utility software — low priced, narrowly focused, and generally useful — will inspire you to simultaneously keep several different programs within easy access.

In certain categories, where the different utilities reviewed provide the same basic functions, you are advised to choose only one. Eliminating confusion is more important than including every possible feature. For example, you could run into trouble if you try to recover files with a backup utility different from the one you used to back them up in the first place.

In other categories, each utility program reviewed performs a unique function, and it may be wise to purchase more than one of them. Disk maintenance is such a category.

The application-specific utilities, such as SOS for Lotus 1-2-3, should reside in the same subdirectory as the main application program.

It is recommended that you keep in one subdirectory the utilities that you will want frequent access to and that are not application-specific. Use the DOS PATH command in your AUTOEXEC.BAT file to provide access to this subdirectory at all times.

The advantages to using the same subdirectory for groups of utilities is that you preserve disk space (each subdirectory takes up disk space of its own), and your DOS PATH command can be short.

However, there are some potential problems with keeping all of your utilities in the same subdirectory. Some utilities create their own sub-directories during the installation process. Some insist on looking for certain file names either in the root directory or in a subdirectory with a specific name.

Many of these utility programs actually consist of several program files that perform related but distinct functions. Consistent with their aim of being fast, economical, and easy to use, the program files tend to have short file names.

Since there are many more utility programs available than letters in the alphabet, some may have identical file names. If you install two files of the same name in the same subdirectory, the first file will overwrite the second. Before installing a new utility program, compare the names of the new files to the files that already exist in that directory. If there are duplicate file names, either install the new files in a different directory or rename one of the files.

If you want to remove a utility program from your disk or install an up-dated version, it may be difficult to ascertain which of the short, cryptic file names pertain to a given utility program. Compare the names of the files you plan to remove with the original program diskette before actually deleting them.

Similarly, if you want to copy all of the files pertaining to a given utility program, you may have to enter several command lines. Using wildcard characters in the COPY command line may not be practical.

RAM Management

In a typical microcomputer, up to 640K RAM is allocated to the user as main memory, and, if available, many additional megabytes of RAM may be allocated to the user as extended or expanded memory. The phrase "allocated to the user" simply means that the user may choose to load software into that space.

Many of the utilities described in this book are used in conjunction with application software; that is, they must be loaded into RAM and be accessible simultaneously with the application software.

These utilities are frequently referred to as **RAM-resident** or **TSRs** (terminate and stay resident) because even when you leave them, they remain in RAM without releasing that memory for use by other software.

Your main application software is referred to as **transient**, since the RAM it uses is released when you exit the application. Most currently available application software requires contiguous RAM for its ancillary overlay files and its active data files.

If you want access to more than one resident utility, you may have several programs in RAM simultaneously.

The loading order of all of this software is important for two reasons:

- space allocation
- input/output servicing

In general, the operating system dictates that software is loaded into main RAM in layers, from the bottom up, on a first-come, first-serve basis. RAM-resident programs should be loaded first, so that the remaining available memory is then open to your main transient applications and their data files. All software should be unloaded in the reverse order in which it was loaded so that no gaps in RAM are created.

You can specify that certain devices, such as print spoolers and RAM disks that cordon off a section of empty RAM for future use, use certain areas of RAM, such as the topmost section of the main memory or a section of extended memory. This specification will leave more RAM available for applications that can address only limited amounts of RAM.

The print spooler or RAM disk program itself, however, is loaded into its layer at the bottom like any other software program.

When you load a file from an application, the application controls where in its available RAM that file is loaded. Data files are usually loaded immediately above the application's program files. If you load another program from within the application, however, the application may unload a portion of itself into **virtual memory**, temporarily allocating the space left to the second program.

Virtual memory is to RAM what RAM is to disks. Information in RAM that is not currently in use — an application's overlay files or the beginning of a long data file, for example — may be temporarily stored on disk space until needed again. Your major concern with virtual memory, however, is that you may not be aware of its use.

Virtual memory is an important consideration when you are running disk maintenance utilities that work directly with all data on your disks. As a rule, no other software should be loaded when using these disk maintenance utilities. Similarly, you should be careful not to erase temporary files (usually with extensions of $$$ or @@@), which you may see if you access your disk from within an application.

For the same reasons, you should not load RAM-resident utilities from within transient applications even if it appears to be possible. The resident utility will not unload, and the application will not be able to reload the information in virtual memory.

The chain of command in input/output operations is the other issue to consider in determining loading order.

If you have loaded more than one resident utility, a permanent chain is formed. Most DOS operations are filtered through this chain of programs. When an application needs to read a keyboard entry, it sends a request down the chain of programs loaded below it in RAM. The answer is filtered up through any RAM-resident utilities back to the application.

For this reason, print spoolers, RAM drives, and other peripheral hardware device drivers that do not interfere with keyboard operations may be loaded first. Your keyboard macro utility should be loaded before any other software you want to filter through it. Most RAM-resident utilities recommend specific loading orders vis-à-vis other RAM-resident utilities. Other loading orders will depend on your individual preference.

Documentation

The user's manuals for these utility programs are often the best educational tool for learning about your hardware, your operating system, and your applications. Many of these manuals take great pains to explain how these programs work in conjunction with other elements of your computer system.

The Utilities

The utility programs reviewed in this book generally fall into one of four levels of complexity:

- simplifying a task for nontechnically oriented computer users

- simplifying a routine task for novices as well as technically oriented users

- providing a tool for a more technically oriented user to set up a user-friendly interface for nontechnically oriented users

- providing extended functions for technically oriented users

The utility programs presented do not make up a comprehensive list of available utilities, as a catalog would contain. The programs that are reviewed here were selected by the criteria of usefulness, popularity, availability, and coverage of important functions. This list is limited by a desire to avoid repetition.

However, in general, the overviews of the functions and utilities are intended to help you choose among and take advantage of the software reviewed, other software not reviewed, and software yet to be published.

CHAPTER 1

DISK MAINTENANCE UTILITIES

Disk maintenance utilities often seem to perform miracles. Their features can help you recover from your worst disk disasters. **Disk maintenance** refers primarily to hard disk maintenance. Hard disks require more care than floppy diskettes for several reasons:

- The larger capacity of a hard disk allows it to contain more data that is important to computer operations.

- A hard disk is used much more frequently than any individual diskette; therefore, it is more vulnerable to user error.

- The relatively delicate construction and mechanical operation of a hard disk drive also makes hard disks more vulnerable to hardware problems.

Hard disk maintenance emphasizes prevention and cure of the causes of problems as well as the recovery of data lost due to mishaps.

Several utilities dealing primarily with file management also include features that overlap with disk maintenance and vice versa. (Also see Chapter 2, "File Management Utilities.")

To understand the types of problems addressed in disk maintenance, you must first understand how information is physically laid out on a disk.

DISK LAYOUT

Conceptually, floppy diskettes and hard disks work in the same way. A disk is actually a flat, circular platter similar to a phonograph record. The surface is coated with material that allows it to be read from and written to by a magnetized drive head. There are two drive heads for each platter, so both sides of the platter may be used. A hard disk consists of two or more of these platters.

Information is written on **tracks** or concentric circular bands on the surface of the disk. The number of tracks depends on the type of disk. A double-density floppy diskette has forty tracks per side, numbered 0-39. A high-density 5-1/4" diskette has eighty tracks per side. A 10-megabyte hard disk contains 306 tracks on each platter. In hard disk terminology, the word **cylinder** refers to each set of tracks with the same radius; a 10-megabyte hard disk with 2 two-sided platters contains four tracks per cylinder.

Each track is further divided into units of space that can be addressed by a single read or write operation of a drive head. These units of space are called **sectors**. Each DOS sector can hold 512 characters (or bytes) of information.

DOS allocates space to files in groups of sectors called **clusters**. No more than one file may be assigned to each cluster. Even a file consisting of a single character is allocated an entire cluster.

A file may be assigned to more than one cluster, depending on its size. When a new file is written to a disk, the first available cluster is used. If more than one cluster is required, the next available cluster is assigned, which may or may not be physically located near the first cluster.

The number of sectors in a cluster is predetermined by the type of disk and, in the case of hard disks, the version of DOS used to format the disk, as shown in the following table:

Medium	DOS version	Tracks per side	Sectors per track	Sectors per cluster
double-density diskette	1.x	40	8	1
double-density diskette	2.x or later	40	9	2
high-density diskette	3.x	80	15	1
10-megabyte hard disk	2.x	306	17	8
20-megabyte hard disk	2.x	616	17	16
20-megabyte hard disk	3.x	616	17	4

All else being equal, a lower number of sectors per cluster means more clusters per disk. Since there may be no more than one file per cluster, the more clusters per disk, the greater the number of files that can occupy the disk.

On the other hand, the lower the number of sectors per cluster, the greater the chance that large files will become fragmented, i.e., spread out in noncontiguous disk areas.

The FORMAT Command

The DOS FORMAT command must be used to initialize each disk before it can hold data. The same FORMAT command is used for all disks, but it behaves somewhat differently for hard disks than for floppy diskettes.

4

On a floppy diskette, sector divisions are physically marked off during the FORMAT operation. The new sectors are filled, and any previous data on the diskette is overwritten with ASCII code 229, which indicates to the computer that the space is empty.

Hard disks are usually formatted with sector divisions before they are installed. The DOS FORMAT command does not physically format or overwrite file data on a hard disk; it passes over the entire disk, checking for and recording any bad sectors so data will not be written to them.

From this point on, the FORMAT command behaves identically for floppy diskettes and hard disks. Three items are written to the disk, beginning with the first sector on the first track on the first side:

- The **boot record** occupies the first sector.

- Two copies of the **file allocation table** (FAT) each occupy two sectors (one sector in DOS version 1.x), beginning on the first sector after the boot record.

- The **root directory** of the disk occupies the next seven sectors on a double-sided diskette or the next 16 sectors on a hard disk.

Storage space for files follows the root directory. If the /S switch is entered on the FORMAT command line, the two system files and the COMMAND.COM file are copied to the first clusters immediately following the root directory.

The Boot Record

The **boot record** is used during the DOS start-up procedure. It contains instructions for loading DOS into RAM. If the computer finds a valid boot record on the default disk (the diskette in drive A or, if drive A is empty, the hard disk), it loads the boot record into RAM and searches for the system files.

If a valid boot record does not exist on the first sector, the process will not continue. If the boot record exists, but system files are not found immediately following the root directory, an error message is displayed. The process is suspended until you press a key instructing the computer to try again. If the boot record is damaged, your computer is unable to pass control to DOS.

The File Allocation Record

The **FAT** is a map of disk clusters containing information DOS uses to locate a file to read or free space on which a file can be written. Each FAT entry corresponds to a cluster and contains one of the following pieces of information about the corresponding cluster:

- The cluster contains a bad sector and is unusable.

- The cluster is available for new data.

- The cluster contains file data; the file ends in this cluster.

- The code for the location of the next cluster assigned to the file and the cluster contain file data.

Two copies of the FAT are maintained on each disk. Both are updated each time a file is created, modified, or deleted. If they do not agree, DOS recognizes a problem and, if possible, attempts to correct it. If a bad sector has developed in one of the tables, DOS will be unable to correct it and will have difficulty locating files.

The Root Directory

The **root directory** is the disk's main table of contents. It differs from subdirectories (see Chapter 3, "Path Utilities") in that its location and maximum size are fixed when the disk is intially formatted.

Each directory entry is 32 bytes long; therefore, each 512-byte sector of a directory can hold up to 16 entries. A double-sided, 360K diskette can contain a maximum of 112 entries (files and/or subdirectories) in the root directory. A hard disk's root directory can hold a maximum of 512 entries.

The directory is the interface between the user and the file allocation table. You cannot directly address the file allocation table through DOS; instead, the file is located through the directory. Each directory entry contains two bytes of information indicating the starting cluster of the file. Once this information is known, the FAT can find the remainder of the file. If the directory is damaged, the files cannot be located.

DISK PROBLEMS

Several types of problems, for which DOS provides little or no assistance, may occur with each of these areas of information (the boot record, the root directory, and the file allocation table):

- lost data due to user error

- lost access to data or damaged data due to bad sectors on a disk

- orphaned data due to errors in the file allocation table

- inefficient disk operation due to fragmented files and subdirectories

- misplaced data due to forgotten file names or incorrect directory designations

Lost Data

Data may be lost when you accidentally delete a file you want to keep, which can easily happen if you use wildcards with the DOS DEL or ERASE commands.

When you or a program you are using instructs DOS to delete a file, DOS performs the following operations:

- DOS replaces the first byte in the directory entry—which contains the first letter of the file name—with ASCII code 229, which indicates to DOS that the entry is available for a new file.

- DOS replaces the FAT entries corresponding to clusters used by the file with codes indicating that the clusters have been freed for new information.

Note that the data itself is not destroyed until new file data is assigned to the freed clusters. Once the directory and FAT entries have been designated as "free," no DOS commands can gain access to the data.

Data may also be lost when you accidentally format the wrong disk, which usually happens when you intend to format a floppy diskette in a different drive and the FORMAT command is stored on the hard disk. If you neglect to enter a drive parameter after the FORMAT command, the default drive is assumed.

Recall that when a floppy diskette is reformatted, all data is overwritten and destroyed. When a hard disk is reformatted, however, data files are not destroyed.

When a hard disk is reformatted, the previous boot record, file allocation table, root directory, and system files are destroyed when the new information is written over them, but all other data remain on the disk. After reformatting, this data is inaccessible to and unprotected by DOS, and it will be overwritten as new information is added to the reformatted disk.

Damaged Data

Data may be lost or damaged due to bad sectors on a disk. This problem is not common when using floppy diskettes; it occurs much more frequently with hard disks. When a hard disk drive is operating, the drive heads are restrained from hitting the spinning platters by a cushion of air. If a foreign particle disturbs this equilibrium or if the computer is subject to jarring or vibration, the heads may "crash" against the platters, disturbing the magnetic coating.

Most hard disks "park" the drive heads over empty areas of the platters before turning the power off, so no data is destroyed when the heads land. Sometimes this parking function is automatic; in other cases, you must manually enter a command to park the heads. If your computer has no parking facility, or you choose not to use it, you may damage data by simply turning the power off and on.

Bad sectors are detected when DOS cannot read information written to the sector, or when the information read does not agree with the information originally written. The latter condition is checked by a value entered at the end of each sector written to the disk. This value is computed from the values of each of the characters written to the sector. When the computer reads the data, it recomputes this value and compares it to the original.

The degree of damage may vary. The sector may be partly readable. The hardware may be usable even if the data is not. The impact of the damage depends on the type of data that is unreadable. Damage to the boot record, FAT, root directory, or any subdirectory can be disastrous. Text files can usually be reconstructed with ease. Program files may not be operable, but you can probably restore them from backup files.

Other types of data files for different applications may be partially salvageable, depending on the application. For example, Lotus 1-2-3 worksheet files will probably not load unless the entire file is intact. On the other hand, dBASE III data base files will load as long as the file header is readable, although damaged records may contain nonsensical symbols.

The DOS RECOVER command provides assistance for problems due to bad sectors. RECOVER can be used on a single file or on an entire disk. If you specify a file name, DOS will create a file of the same name, consisting of all information (possibly including extraneous data after the file's end) in the undamaged 512-byte sectors allocated to the file.

The damaged sector will be omitted entirely. The damaged cluster will be labeled as unusable on the FAT. If you can use the damaged sector, copy the original file to a new file before using the RECOVER command on the original file. You should still RECOVER the original file, if only for the purpose of removing the damaged sector from future use.

Using the DOS RECOVER command on an entire disk is a formidable task. All files, including subdirectories, will be rewritten to the root directory of the same disk, according to the information in the file allocation table. Each recovered file will have the name "file ####.rec," where #### is a sequential number distinguishing each file. There will be no other indication of the original file type.

Orphaned Data

Data may be cut off from its file assignment as a result of hardware error or a program error causing the computer to "lock up" between a disk write operation and the file allocation table update.

Depending on the specific cause of the problem and the response of the program running at the time, the file in question may or may not be usable.

If you encounter no other file problems, you may remain unaware of this floating data. The data's cluster assignment is not freed, thereby shortchanging you on disk space. Also, you may be missing valuable information and be unaware that is gone.

The DOS CHKDSK command will report "lost" clusters or chains. **Lost clusters**, according to DOS, are clusters allocated according to the FAT but not belonging to any file. A **lost chain** is a contiguous group of lost clusters. DOS will not report any information on data in clusters available according to the FAT.

The /F switch, when used with the the DOS CHKDSK command, allows you to convert lost chains of clusters to separate files or to free up the FAT entry. If you choose to convert the clusters, the new file or files will be named "file ####.chk," where #### is a sequential number distinguishing each file. You can then examine the data in the new file or files to determine if further action is necessary.

Inefficient Disk Access

Recall that files are assigned to clusters according to the next available space determined by the file allocation table. If no space is available in prior clusters and sufficient space is available immediately following the first cluster assigned to the file, the file is allocated to sequential, contiguous clusters.

This tidy situation, however, is not always the case. Suppose, for example, that you write a second file to the disk, delete a previously written file, and then add data to the first file. The second file may be allocated to the cluster immediately following the first file. The cluster formerly containing the deleted file is freed.

The first file is then assigned additional clusters located either after the second file or where the deleted file formerly existed. In either case, the entire first file is no longer located in contiguous clusters.

Certain types of files are much more likely to become fragmented than others. Small files such as batch files, which are no larger than one cluster, never present such a problem. Similarly, executable program files, which are rarely modified once installed, remain as contiguous as they were when first installed. Large, frequently modified data files are most likely to become fragmented in noncontiguous clusters across the disk.

The presence of fragmented files slows disk access considerably while the drive heads move from track to track looking for the next assigned cluster. Fragmented files are also more difficult to reconstruct in case of accidental erasure, since various pieces of the file may be located anywhere on the disk.

The DOS CHKDSK command followed by a file specification will report the number of noncontiguous clusters allocated to a specified file; however, CHKDSK will do nothing to remedy the situation.

Empty subdirectory entries also increase disk access time. Space allocated to subdirectories is not reclaimed when subdirectory entries are deleted. DOS must search each subdirectory entry in a path, whether or not it is actively assigned to a file. These free entry slots may be used by new files. If the entries are not reused, however, you may be wasting valuable disk space and valuable disk access time.

The best solution DOS offers to these problems is that you copy the files to another disk, reformat the disk, and copy the files back.

Misplaced Data

The last problem to be discussed is more of a human problem than a hardware problem. As you add files to your disks, they become more difficult to track. There are many methods of organizing your files to assist in this area (see Chapter 2, "File Management Utilities" and Chapter 3, "Path Utilities"). Even the best organization, however, is no guarantee that you will be able to locate the information you need.

For example, you may need to recall a document file containing a reference to a specific subject, and you may not recall which file contains the reference. The DOS solution is to examine each file individually, using your application program or the DOS TYPE command.

A different but related situation may occur when you remember a file name but cannot find the file in the disk and directory in which you thought it was located. The file may have been inadvertently deleted, but it also may have been inadvertently placed in another directory or on another diskette. The DOS solution to this problem is to list all the directories using either the DIR or TREE commands until you find the file.

Disk maintenance utilities described in this chapter provide alternative methods for addressing all of these problems. The utilities address the deeper issues of preventative maintenance, often rectifying the cause of problems. Some provide shortcuts to DOS solutions, while others provide solutions to problems that cannot be solved by DOS. These programs are essential supplements to your DOS utilities.

DISK MAINTENANCE STRATEGY

There are three basic steps associated with each problem addressed by disk maintenance:

- preventing the problems and their potentially disastrous impact

- curing the cause of the problems

- recovering the lost or damaged data

Prevention

The first rule of prevention is to back up your files (see Chapter 12, "Backup Utilities"). Routine backups can alleviate some of these problems. The existence of backup files at least ensures that hard disk problems need not have a disastrous impact; however, backup files are only part of the solution.

The second rule of prevention is to address problems immediately. An accidentally deleted file may be fully recovered if nothing has been written to the disk since the deletion. A disk reformatted by mistake may be fully recovered if nothing else has been written to the disk since the FORMAT command was entered. A program file damaged by a bad sector will not cause damage to your data files if the corrupted program is not run.

In all these cases, the more you continue to use your computer after the error occurrs, the less data will be recoverable. Even if you continue your computer operations, you may still be able to recover part of your information. Partial recovery is often, though not always, better than none.

The third rule of prevention is to perform routine check-ups of your disks, through which you may detect problems before they interfere with your operations or affect files.

You should develop a habit of regularly using the DOS CHKDSK command to discover orphaned data and noncontinguous files, and you should regularly use disk test programs of the utilities in this book to locate and seal off bad sectors.

Finally, use one of the disk maintenance utilities to preserve the structural elements of your data, i.e., the boot sector, root directory, and file allocation table. These are the elements that, if recoverable, can make other data recovery much easier.

Cure

Even securely protected data can encounter problems. Accidents do happen. An act of God or another well-meaning person may damage your data.

Merely restoring data from your backup files does little to address the problem causing the damage in the first place.

If the problem was caused by a disk error, it will probably recur with the restored files unless the disk is repaired. Obviously, if damage is caused by some external factor (for example, power surges or vibration), these factors must be eliminated.

The most important "curing" operation is sealing off bad sectors. The DOS FORMAT command seals off bad sectors found during the FORMAT procedure before any data is written to the disk. The DOS RECOVER command seals off bad sectors if they are allocated to a specific file or files and you know the name of the file or files. Some disk maintenance utilities described in this book provide disk repair functions that perform more functions than the DOS commands.

There is no permanent cure for inefficient disk access. The more data you store in your computer, the more time it takes to access the data; however, the arrangement of files can be controlled and fragmentation kept to a minimum.

Renaming the format program and running it from a batch file that insists on receiving a drive parameter can eliminate accidental formats of your hard disk.

Renaming files and reorganizing the path environment can keep files in the correct directory and make them easier to identify.

Recovery

Restoring a complete, recent set of backup files to the hard disk often results in full data recovery. Even the directory structure can be re-created with this operation.

Some data, however, cannot be recovered by simply restoring backup files. For example, backup files cannot restore data written to the disk after the most recent backup. On the other hand, the more recently the backup files were created, the more likely it is that the backup files contain the same damaged data as the original disk.

The advantage of disk maintenance utilities is that data is often more easily recovered using less comprehensive measures.

Begin data recovery with the simplest available method. If the first attempt does not work, move on to the next simplest method, and so on. Leave the most complex methods for last. The more complex an operation, the more work is involved in completing the recovery operation.

THE UTILITIES

Each disk maintenance utility described in this book offers a unique combination of maintenance tools. The tools that directly address the problems already discussed in this chapter will be described next. Many of these utilities include other handy features mentioned only in the review of the specific program.

Lost Data Due to User Error

Several disk maintenance utilities provide a function to recover accidentally deleted files in the following ways:

1. Choose the file from a list of deleted directory entries that have not yet been reused.

2. Name the recovered file.

3. Locate the starting cluster of the file according to the remaining information in the directory entry.

4. Guess the following clusters. Usually, this operation merely selects the next unallocated, contiguous clusters.

5. Search for specific data not found in the previous step.

6. Write the recovered file to the disk and update the directory and FAT.

Files recovered in this manner should be reviewed before they are used since extraneous data may be picked up, data may be omitted, or data may be in the wrong order.

Note: a deleted file cannot be recovered once its directory entry has been reused.

Utilities that recover deleted files may allow you to recover removed subdirectories, which makes it possible to then recover deleted files formerly in those subdirectories.

Another major data recovery feature is the ability to undo an accidental hard disk FORMAT command. You will recall that formatting a hard disk does not physically destroy the file data on the disk; it merely removes the information DOS uses to locate the files.

There are two ways a format recovery may be performed by these utility programs. The first method takes advantage of structural information stored in a file by the utility *before* the FORMAT command is entered. If available, this method is the easiest and most likely to succeed. Obviously, this file may only be used if you have the foresight to store the structural information in the first place.

The second method is similar to the process used by the DOS RECOVER command, but the process is reversed. The RECOVER command uses the FAT to locate the clusters belonging to the files. The FORMAT command destroys the data in the FAT. These utilities examine the clusters and use the data in them to reconstruct the FAT. The recovered files are named in the same manner as with the RECOVER command; they are given nondescriptive, sequentially numbered file names.

Compatibility is a larger issue with the Undo feature than with other categories because of differences in the FORMAT commands of various operating systems and disk types.

Lost or Damaged Data Due to Bad Sectors

Many disk maintenance utilities locate and seal off bad sectors. They may improve on DOS in any combination of the following ways:

- In contrast to the FORMAT command, the utilities can be used at any time, without disturbing information on the disk.

- In contrast to the RECOVER command, the utilities can repair areas of the disk not currently allocated to a file.

- The utilities may have higher standards than DOS commands for determining if a sector is fit for use.

- The utilities may provide the option of displaying or printing the damaged information, enabling you to reconstruct it.

- The utilities automatically remove data from bad sectors and seal those sectors off.

It is recommended that you allow these utilities to make more than one pass across the hard disk so that intermittent errors are more likely to be detected. Higher standards frequently result in additional sectors being marked as unusable. On a hard disk with many megabytes of memory, the relatively small loss of capacity is much less important than the safety of your data.

Orphaned Data Due to FAT Errors

The main problem in dealing with orphaned data is determining where it originated. DOS can only provide access to this data by converting it to files. Some disk maintenance utilities, however, allow you to view data by physical location or sector as well as by file name.

Once the data is accessible, it still may be difficult to read. If it is text data and you use CHKDSK to convert it into a file, you may use the DOS TYPE command to view it. If it is not text data, it may be unreadable.

Another feature provided by some of these utilities is alternate display formats, usually hexadecimal or ASCII. Most program files contain at least some textual data, even if it is only a copyright notice. Even a novice may be able to determine the source of the orphaned data by viewing it in ASCII format.

Inefficient Disk Access

Several utility programs can reorganize the data on your disk for more efficient access. The DOS method consists of backing up files, reformatting the disk, and copying the files back to the disk. These utilities improve on the DOS method in the following ways:

- The entire process can be performed with one command line.

- The reorganization takes place entirely on one disk. It is not necessary to copy files between disks.

●   The reorganization automatically allocates space according to file type in a manner designed to minimize subsequent fragmentation. Subdirectories are located closest to the root directory. Executable files follow because they are the least likely to be modified. Application data files, which are the most likely to be modified, are placed last.

●   Once reorganization has been performed, subsequent defragmentation can be accomplished in a fraction of the time.

●   Some programs provide you with the option of determining the organizational logic. You may specify the order or location of various types of files.

●   Subdirectories are automatically condensed, eliminating space allocated to unused directory entries.

Misplaced Data

Finding misplaced data is more a function of file management than disk maintenance; however, many of these disk maintenance utilities include features to assist you in locating misplaced data.

Additional assistance in finding data is provided by various features in disk maintenance utilities. In contrast to a DOS file search, you may be able to search for a given file specification in every subdirectory with a single command line.

Another available function is the ability to search for specific text or data, as mentioned previously. Such a search may be performed by file or by disk sector.

Compatibility

Many disk maintenance utility features may be applied to floppy diskettes as well as hard disks.

Most of these extensive operations are not compatible, however, with RAM-resident, concurrent, or multi-user operations.

The specific features of each utility program are described in the following sections.

DFIXER

MicroWay
P.O. Box 79
Kingston, Massachusetts 02364
Telephone: (617) 746-7341

Software Features

Lost or Damaged Data Due to Bad Sectors

DFixer performs one task well; it examines every sector on a hard disk. Unused sectors are tested for both read and write operations. If a bad sector is found in an unallocated area, the cluster containing the sector is marked as unusable on the FAT and reported to you.

Sectors currently occupied by file data are read-tested only. If a bad sector is found in an area allocated to a valid file, the FAT is not altered, but DFixer reports the error. In this case, you should try to salvage the file with the DOS COPY command unless you have a perfectly good backup copy. If this is the case, you may delete the file and run DFixer again. If the sector tests as "bad" after the space has been unallocated, DFixer will seal it off by marking it unusable in the FAT.

User Interface

DFixer is run with a simple, one-word command from the DOS prompt. The screen display reports the progress as the program runs.

DISK OPTIMIZER

SoftLogic Solutions, Inc.
One Perimeter Road
Manchester, New Hampshire 03103
Telephone: (603) 627-9900
Sales: (800) 272-9900

Software Features

Inefficient Disk Operation

Of the utilities reviewed here, Disk Optimizer offers the most comprehensive solution to fragmented files.

The Analyze function analyzes your disk files to determine the level of
fragmentation. You may analyze a single file, a group of files with
wildcard file specifications, a directory, or an entire disk. This feature
is useful in determining how frequently to run the Optimize function.

The Optimize function will automatically reallocate files in sequence,
closing all gaps to minimize subsequent fragmentation. Optimize can be
configured to organize files according to your specifications.

Subdirectories are automatically listed as the first entries of their parent
directories. You may specify the order in which your directories will be
listed. You may also specify file name extensions you consider to be
"static." Since these files are rarely modified, they will be placed first
in the optimized layout. Alternatively, you can specify that the static
files should be placed together at the end of the disk, which may be
more efficient for a disk that is over half full. Hidden files are never
moved.

Lost or Damaged Data Due to Bad Sectors

The Optimize program also detects bad sectors on a disk. If part of a
file is unreadable, a message and, optionally, a report file, is reported to
the screen. If an unused sector is unreadable, the FAT will be updated
so the sector will not be allocated to future files.

Other Features

Disk Optimizer's Filepeek function allows you to view data in any file in four different formats: hexadecimal, ASCII, simultaneous hexadecimal and ASCII, or line text format.

File security features allow you to encrypt a file or group of files with wildcard file specifications so that such files are accessible only by password.

User Interface

Most of the features in Disk Optimizer may be run either in interactive mode or as command lines from the DOS prompt. Messages are displayed as each program is run.

DSRECOVER

Design Software, Inc.
1275 West Roosevelt Road
West Chicago, Illinois 60185
Telephone: (312) 231-4540

Software Features

DSRECOVER is a user-friendly, RAM-resident utility designed to prevent permanent data loss due to user error.

Lost Data Due to User Error

DSRECOVER is for computer users with foresight. Protected data may be recovered from accidental deletion or accidental reformat.

When DSRECOVER is activated, you may delete files, but their directory positions and FAT entries are not freed for new files. With this precaution taken, DSRECOVER will always be able to recover the file. You may "purge" or remove the protection from protected deleted files to free up disk space. Files may be purged or recovered singly, by wildcard file specification, by directory, or by drive.

DSRECOVER also includes a feature to save the structural elements of your hard disk's format — the boot sector, file allocation table, and root directory — to a file. If your hard disk is accidentally reformatted, this file may be used to restore the structural elements. The more recently this file was saved and the fewer changes made since saving it, the more accurate your unformatted disk will be.

User Interface

DSRECOVER uses a Lotus-style menu. The major part of the screen is occupied by a display of the protected files, which may be scrolled to view additional files. On-line help is available.

DSRECOVER features can also be run as command lines from the DOS prompt.

MACE + UTILITIES

Paul Mace Software
123 North First Street
Ashland, Oregon 97520
Telephone: (503) 488-0224

Software Features

Mace+ Utilities address some of the most serious error messages DOS can generate and can help correct the worst catastrophes you may bring upon yourself.

Lost Data Due to User Error

Mace+ includes routines to recover an accidentally deleted file as well as an accidentally reformatted disk.

The Undelete feature allows you to select a file from a list of deleted files whose directory entries have not yet been reused. The probable condition of the file is indicated with a simple comparison of the file size (provided by the directory entry) and the amount of unallocated contiguous space following the starting sector (also provided by the directory entry).

It is recommended that you recover the file to a different drive. Recovered files may span more than one diskette; the parts may be concatenated with the DOS COPY command.

Once you indicate the first character of the file name, you may view the contents of any cluster and choose whether or not to include it in the recovered file.

Two methods are provided for unformatting a reformatted disk. The first method restores backup copies of the boot sector, FAT, and root directory made by the Mace + RXBAK feature *if* you have the foresight to use this feature. The accuracy of the recovery depends on how recently the backup copies have been updated.

The second method, Unformat, is the next best option. Unformat will recover all subdirectories and the files in them. Fragmented files will probably not be recovered accurately. The files you want to save must then be copied to another disk, and the hard disk must be reformatted again.

Lost or Damaged Data Due to Bad Sectors

Mace + includes several routines to assist in diagnosing, repairing, and recovering from bad sectors on a disk. The Diagnose feature may be run independently or with the Remedy feature. Reclaim is a separate, last-resort option.

Diagnose will make as many passes as you choose over all disk sectors. The standards used by Diagnose to determine bad sectors are higher than the standards used by DOS. If part of a file is unreadable, a copy of the readable portion is reported to the screen, printer, and/or a report file.

Remedy will update the FAT to include bad sectors reported during Diagnose. In addition, this feature will move the data to an undamaged area of the disk so you may examine and attempt to reconstruct your file.

Reclaim is a drastic measure with results similar to, but potentially more accurate than, the DOS RECOVER command. The accuracy of the results depends on how well Mace + can reconstruct the FAT. The files must be recovered to a separate disk. You may format diskettes "on the fly." Recovered files may span more than one diskette; the parts may be concatenated with the DOS COPY command.

Restoring backup information saved by RXBAK may also be used if any of the structural elements — boot sector, root directory, or file allocation table — have been damaged.

Inefficient Disk Operation

Mace + offers two features to address inefficient disk access due to fragmented files and inflated subdirectories.

The Condense function will automatically reallocate files in sequence, closing all gaps to minimize subsequent fragmentation. Condense automatically stores read-only files first because they are least likely to be modified in the future.

Mace + also offers a feature to close up and sort directories, eliminating the need for DOS to search deleted entries. References to directories within directories are listed first, followed by files in the order you select (by name, extension, date and time, or size.)

User Interface

Mace + is primarily menu-driven. An informative map of disk space is updated, and messages are displayed as each program is run. On-line help is available.

Some of the features, such as Diagnose, Remedy, and Condense, can also be run as a command line from the DOS prompt.

Diagnostic reports and dumps of damaged clusters may be reported to the screen, printer, and/or a report file. The reports are available through either the menu or command-line interface.

THE NORTON UTILITIES

Peter Norton Computing, Inc.
2210 Wilshire Boulevard, #186
Santa Monica, California 90403
Telephone: (213) 453-2361

Software Features

The Norton Utilities are a collection of disk maintenance programs addressing data recovery. In addition, they contain several routines useful for file management.

Lost Data Due to User Error

The Unerase feature allows you to select a file from a list of deleted files whose directory entries have not yet been reused. The potential for recovery depends on whether the starting cluster (provided by the directory entry) has been reallocated to another file.

After you indicate the first character of the file name, you may view the contents of any cluster and choose whether or not to include it in the recovered file.

The Norton Utilities also offer a Quick Unerase command that completely automates this process, guessing by location which data to include in the recovered files.

The Unremove feature allows you to recover a subdirectory that has been removed. This feature is particularly useful if you need to Unerase a file formerly in that subdirectory.

Lost or Damaged Data Due to Bad Sectors

The Norton Utilities provide two tests for diagnosing problems on your disk. The Disk Read test reads every sector of the disk, whether or not the sector is allocated to a file. The File Read test reads every file and directory.

If part of a file is unreadable, a message is reported to the screen and, optionally, a report file. If an unused sector is unreadable, the FAT will be updated so the sector will not be allocated to future files.

Other Features

The Norton Utilities include features very useful for locating specific files and data. A File Find function lists all files in any directory (indicating the directory) that match a given file specification. A Text Search function will search files and/or the entire disk for a given string of text.

Other file management features include sorting subdirectories according to user specification, changing file attributes, and summarizing the amount of space allocated to a file or group of files.

The Norton Utilities contain several other useful features in miscellaneous categories beyond the scope of this book.

User Interface

Most of the Norton Utilities may be run either in interactive mode or as command lines from the DOS prompt. Messages are displayed as each program is run. On-line help is available.

The results of several of the programs may be reported to the screen, printer, and/or a report file. The reports are available through either the interactive or command line mode.

Other Software in this Category

DISK TECHNICIAN

Prime Solutions Inc.
1940 Garnet Avenue
San Diego, California 92109
Telephone: (619) 274-5000

DISK EXPLORER

Quaid Software Limited
45 Charles Street East, Third Floor
Toronto, Ontario, Canada M4Y 1S2
Telephone: (416) 961-8243

PC TOOLS

Central Point Software, Inc.
9700 SW Capitol Highway, Suite 100
Portland, Oregon 97219-9978
Telephone: (503) 244-5782

UTILITIES I/UTILITIES III

IBM Personally Developed Software
PO Box 3280
Wallingford, Connecticut 06494-3280
Telephone: (800) 426-7279

DISK P.M.

Digital Pathways, Inc.
201 Ravendale Drive
Mountain View, California 94043
Telephone: (415) 964-0707

CHAPTER 2

FILE MANAGEMENT UTILITIES

File management might also be referred to as directory management, since directories are the means to accessing computer files. An understanding of directories and subdirectories is the most important element of file management.

A **directory** is like a table of contents for your computer files. In a directory, each file has a line entry containing the following information:

- the file name and extension

- the number of bytes of disk space allocated to the file

- the date and time the file was created or last modified

- the attribute flags (hidden, system, archive, or read-only file, volume label, or subdirectory)

- the disk location for the beginning of the file

As you can see from the possible attribute flags, a directory entry may represent a file, a volume label for the directory, or a subdirectory.

The two types of directories—the **root** directory and **subdirectories**—serve similar purposes and are accessed in a similar manner. The principal differences are as follows:

- There is only one root directory, while there may be many subdirectories.

- The root directory is created automatically during the FORMAT command and cannot be removed, while subdirectories must be explicitly created and deleted.

- The size of the root directory, and, therefore, the maximum number of entries in the root directory, is fixed; subdirectories are not fixed in size or number of entries.

- The root directory is always at the top of the hierarchical directory structure, while there may be multiple levels of subdirectories.

All other operations involving directories and their files, such as listing, locating, copying, renaming, and deleting files, are identical for either type of directory.

This discussion of directories and file access pertains to floppy diskettes as well as hard disks. File management pertains to files on floppy diskettes as well as on hard disks; however, these utility programs are especially useful to hard disk users because of the greater number of files maintained on a hard disk.

As mentioned in Chapter 1, several utilities that deal primarily with disk maintenance also include features that overlap with file management, and vice versa.

Subdirectories are very helpful for organizing large numbers of files. DOS provides many tools for working with files in any directory; however, there are many useful file and directory management operations that are cumbersome or impossible with DOS alone.

Some operations on the following "wish list" involve access to single files:

- view or change a file's attributes
- search for a file across directories
- locate a file containing specific text
- view a file's contents
- move a file between directories

VIEW OR CHANGE FILE ATTRIBUTES

The term **attribute** has a precise meaning for DOS files. Files, as previously mentioned, include the following attributes:

- read-only
- hidden
- system
- volume label
- subdirectory
- archive

Each of these attributes is represented by a **bit,** which is set either to 1 (on) or 2 (off). Some of these attributes are, of course, mutually exclusive. For example, if an entry is a volume label, the remaining attributes are meaningless; however, some of the attributes may coexist. For example, a file may simultaneously be a read-only, hidden, system, and archive file. DOS system files usually have all these attributes.

The standard directory listing available with the internal DOS DIR command does not display file attributes, but certain attributes are evident from the directory display. The volume label, if one exists, is displayed at the top of the listing. Subdirectories are designated in the file listing by the notation <DIR> in place of the file size. The remaining attributes are not evident. System and hidden files are not displayed.

Most DOS commands cannot access system or hidden files. Some DOS commands can access read-only files, but only the following limited-purpose DOS commands perform operations on entries with other attributes:

- ATTRIB, an external DOS command available in versions 3 and later, can display or change the read-only attribute for a given file specification.

- VOL, an internal DOS command available in versions 2 and later, can display the label given to a disk or partition on a disk.

- LABEL, an external DOS command available in versions 3 or later, can create, change, or delete a volume label for a disk or partition on a disk.

- MKDIR (MD), CHDIR (CD), and RMDIR (RD), internal DOS commands available in versions 2 or later, respectively create, change, and delete subdirectories.

- BACKUP and RESTORE, external DOS commands available in versions 2 or later, are the only DOS commands that modify or make use of the archive attribute.

SEARCH FOR A FILE ACROSS DIRECTORIES

Accessing files that are neither hidden nor system files is not difficult with DOS as long as you know the file's name and the directory in which it is located. Searching for a file across directories is more difficult. If you want to find a file and do not know its subdirectory, DOS provides two alternatives.

TREE, an external DOS command available in versions 2 and later, reports on all directories and, with the /f parameter, on all nonhidden and nonsystem files in all directories. The output can be scanned as it scrolls or redirected to a printer and scanned for the desired file name; however, no file name specification may be used to limit the number of files reported.

Alternatively, you may search for the desired file by using the DIR command with a specified directory path to list each directory in turn. Each directory listing requires a separate command line. If you know the file name or some part of it, a file specification (including wildcard characters) may be added to the DIR command to limit the search and shorten the output display.

LOCATE A FILE CONTAINING SPECIFIC TEXT

Searching for a file containing specific text is difficult with DOS if you don't know the file name. Two DOS commands, TYPE and FIND, provide minimal assistance, but they are the only DOS commands that read and report the contents of a file. Even with these two commands, searching through a group of files is a cumbersome matter of trial and error, requiring multiple command lines.

TYPE, an internal DOS command, displays the contents of a file and nothing else. The output may be scanned as it scrolls or redirected to a printer and scanned for the desired information. The TYPE command accepts only one file name at a time, and wildcard characters are not acceptable; therefore, searching a group of files requires entering the command line containing the path and file name for each file to be read.

FIND, an external DOS command, reports the occurrence of a specific string of text in a specific file. For this purpose, FIND improves on the TYPE command in two ways. First, you need not read the entire file to find the text. Second, although the path and file name are still required, and wilcard characters are not allowed, you can specify from a single command line to search for more than one file.

VIEW A FILE'S CONTENTS

The DOS TYPE command displays the contents of a file in ASCII format. If the file is not a straight text file, the display will be unreadable. DOS provides the DEBUG program for the purpose of reading and modifying files loaded into RAM in hexadecimal format.

For either of these methods, you must leave your current operation and overwrite information on the display screen, and you must regenerate any of the overwritten information needed after you examine the contents of a particular file.

These methods are acceptable if you are examining one or two specific files, but if you are trying to investigate a group of files from a directory listing, the procedures can be cumbersome.

MOVE A FILE BETWEEN DIRECTORIES

Because subdirectories are such an important organizational tool for file management, you will probably want to occasionally reorganize your files. To reallocate files in subdirectories, you must move files from one directory to another. Using DOS, this apparently simple operation requires two steps. First, you must COPY the file or files you want to move to the new directory. Then, you must DEL or ERASE them from the original directory.

For both of these steps, wildcard characters are allowed; therefore, if you are moving an entire directory or group of files with identical extensions or similar file names, you may be able to use the file specification to limit the number of command lines required to move the group of files.

Other useful file and directory operations that are cumbersome or impossible with DOS involve managing groups of files and the directories, such as the following:

- sorting directory entries by name, extension, date, or size
- renaming a directory
- removing a directory
- viewing directories
- selecting a group of files

SORT DIRECTORY ENTRIES

Files are arranged in directories on a first-come, first-serve basis. After you have modified, deleted, and created new files over a period of time, this order, for all practical purposes, becomes random. Sifting through directory entries can be tiresome. Sorting files by various criteria, such as the following, can be helpful in several situations:

- alphabetically — to find a particular file name
- by extension — to find a particular type of file
- by date — to locate most recent or most obsolete files
- by size — to manage use of disk capacity

DOS provides a flexible (but not very friendly) method for viewing directory entries in a nonrandom order. The DIR command can be "filtered" through SORT, an external DOS command, to reorder the output, which may be displayed on the screen or redirected to a file or printer. To display the listing in alphabetical order, type

DIR ¦ SORT

from the DOS prompt, and press

<return>

Two options available with SORT extend its flexibility. The /R parameter produces the output in reverse. The /+n parameter will sort the output, starting from the nth column. This option can be used to sort the directory listing by extension, size, or date by specifying the column number corresponding to that part of the directory entry:

file name   column 1 (default)
extension   column 10
file size   column 14
file date   column 24

Note, however, that SORT will only sort in ASCII order; therefore, the date order sorts by month, then day, then year, as displayed; 10/01/85 is listed after 03/15/87.

RENAME A DIRECTORY

Subdirectories are named as they are created with the DOS MKDIR or MD command. DOS provides no way to change the name of a subdirectory. You can, however, rename a subdirectory by creating a new subdirectory, copying all files in the old subdirectory to the new subdirectory, deleting all files in the old subdirectory, and removing the old subdirectory. This process involves four command steps:

MKDIR \new   create the new subdirectory.

COPY \old*.* \new   copy all of the files in the old subdirectory to the new subdirectory (this step can be time-consuming).

DEL \old*.*   delete all of the files in the old subdirectory because a directory cannot be removed until it is empty. You will be prompted for confirmation with the message, "Are you sure Y/N?"

RMDIR \old   remove the old subdirectory

REMOVE A DIRECTORY

Note that removing a subdirectory using DOS commands is always a two-step operation. The DEL or ERASE command cannot be used on a subdirectory itself. The command RMDIR or RD must be used to delete a subdirectory. Deleting all files in a subdirectory does not delete the subdirectory; however, a subdirectory must be empty of files before it can be removed.

VIEW DIRECTORIES

Viewing a group of directory entries or the directory structure is hampered by DOS's inability to scroll the output display back and forth. The DIR and TREE commands generate listings of this information. If the listing passes too quickly on the screen, your only option is to reenter the command to display it. There are mechanisms to control the display of these and certain other DOS commands:

- Pressing <Ctrl/NumLock> will freeze the display scroll; pressing any other key will resume the scrolling.

- Entering DIR/W displays only file names and extensions in five columns across the screen. While the directory information is limited, the display contains five times as many file names as a normal directory listing.

- Entering DIR/P displays the normal directory information one screen at a time. When the screen is filled, the listing pauses; pressing any other key will resume the scrolling.

- The redirection symbol can be used to direct the output of a DOS command to a printer (DIR >prn) or to a file (DIR >filename).

- The MORE command can be used with other DOS commands to display one screen at a time (DIR ¦ MORE). When the screen is filled, the listing pauses; pressing any other key will resume the scrolling.

DOS provides no mechanism for scrolling backwards. To view information already passed from the screen, you must reenter the command from the DOS prompt and start again from the beginning of the list.

Furthermore, these DOS commands are mutually exclusive. The file information displayed with the DIR command is confined to files in one directory or subdirectory. The file information displayed with the TREE command spans all directories but is limited to much less information per file than the DIR command. DOS does not allow you to view this information simultaneously.

Examining certain statistics of a group of files is not easy with only the tools provided by DOS. Two commands provide limited information on groups of files:

- DIR, in addition to reporting individual file sizes and dates, reports the number of files in a given directory that match the file name specification.

- CHKDSK, in addition to reporting disk problems, reports the amount of space used by all files on the entire disk.

There are two steps to generating information on a group of files:

- selecting the files to be reported on

- reporting the desired information

Both of these steps can be performed in a limited manner by DOS. For example, suppose you want to know the amount of disk space occupied by a certain group of files, which would be useful information for preparing to back up files onto diskettes or for managing the use of disk space. Neither the DIR nor CHKDSK command can report this information.

SELECT A GROUP OF FILES

The only method of selecting files is to use file name specifications. There is no method to globally select files by any other criterion, e.g., file attribute, and there is no way to individually assign a file to a group.

Furthermore, even if you could select the desired group of files, no DOS command reports the required information. While the DIR command reports individual file sizes in bytes, it does not display a total of bytes used by the group of files listed.

At the other extreme, the CHKDSK command reports the total bytes used by all files on a disk but provides no method of limiting the report to a specific file or group of files. Note that CHKDSK does accept a file name specification parameter, but the function of the parameter is only to specify which files to analyze for allocation to noncontiguous sectors. Even with the file name specification, the CHKDSK command reports the number of bytes used by all files on the disk.

These limitations apply to other standard DOS operations. While some commands may operate on groups of files, others cannot. Even those commands that can operate on groups of files, such as COPY, DEL, or RENAME, will accept only a file name specification as a criterion.

The file management utilities discussed here provide simultaneous access to all files, allowing organization, analysis, and search functions not available with DOS and enhancing those operations that DOS does provide.

FILE MANAGEMENT STRATEGY

In general, file management is the efficient arrangement of files on a disk. Its implementation is primarily the responsibility of the computer user. There are four elements of file organization that determine the efficiency of file management:

- file names
- directory organization
- file attributes
- currency of data

File naming is a much more important element of file management than most computer users initially realize. The most obvious reason for foresight in file naming is to identify the file's contents in a meaningful way to help you

- recall the name when you need access to the file

- recognize the name when you view a group of files.

A more subtle but equally important reason is the ability to access a group of files by file name specification in conjunction with wildcard characters. For example, if all your document files pertaining to project A are named PROJA1.DOC, PROJA2.DOC, and so on, you can view a directory consisting of only these files by typing

```
DIR PROJA*.DOC
```

from the DOS prompt and then pressing

```
<return>
```

Many other DOS operations can be performed in the same manner on a group of files.

As mentioned previously, file name specification is the only way to group files with DOS commands. Even with the utility programs discussed in this chapter (and other categories of utility programs), file name specification is a primary means of addressing a group of files.

Directory organization is also an important tool of file management. Subdirectories originated as tools for managing large numbers of files. There are two considerations when organizing large numbers of files into separate subdirectories based on user, application, or file type:

- You can use the subdirectory path in much the same way you use a file name specification to select a group of files.

- It is much easier to access a number of files in the same directory than to access a group of files across two or more directories.

As mentioned previously, most DOS commands cannot access files in different directories simultaneously (see Chapter 3, "Path Utilities"). Similarly, even the utility programs described in this chapter (and other categories of utility programs) perform better with files in the same directory than with files in different directories.

File attributes can be used to supplement file name specifications as tools for controlling access to various files. For example, hidden files will not appear in a directory listing, limiting the number of file entries you must scan to find the file you need. The archive attribute can be used by the BACKUP and RESTORE commands alone or in conjunction with a file name and/or date specification to limit the number of files copied by either command.

Unfortunately, DOS does not provide any easy ways to modify, or even ascertain, a file's attributes, as previously mentioned. The ATTRIB command, available in DOS 3.0 and later versions, works only with the read-only attribute. The BACKUP command resets the archive attribute.

Further modification of file attributes is not available through standard DOS commands; however, changing a file's attributes is one area in which the utilities described in this chapter excel.

You should proceed with care, however, in changing file attributes because they may provide protection from accidental deletion or modification. Do not "unhide" hidden files unless you must remove them. Do not "hide" files which may require standard DOS command access. Make backup copies of read-only files before removing the read-only attribute. Reset the read-only attribute after modifying the file. Do not make frequently changed files read-only files.

The final element of file management is to keep only currently-used files on your disk. Temporary, obsolete, or superfluous files should be promptly deleted or removed to diskettes for storage to

- free up precious disk space

- reduce the opportunity for inadvertent access to the wrong file

- reduce directory clutter to make it easier to find the files you need

There are two aspects of file management, as opposed to the end result, that can have a great impact on achieving and maintaining this efficiency:

- visualization of directory structure and contents

- ease of file operations

One problem when working with computer files is the inability to actually see what you are doing. The physical appearance of a disk provides no information. Your monitor and, to some extent, your printer, provide a visual display of your computer operations; however, monitors are typically only 80 characters wide and 24 lines long; therefore, they can display only limited information at any given moment.

A graphic picture of your directory structure and a display of the directory's contents can be helpful when making file management decisions. The tools DOS offers in this area and their limitations have already been discussed. The utilities described in this book excel in the area of visual presentation.

Additionally, the easier it is for you to perform file operations, the more likely it is that you will manage your files efficiently. While most elements of efficient file management can be accomplished with the tools provided by DOS, the utilities described in this chapter expand the options and make the process easier.

THE UTILITIES

File management utilities, in the context of this chapter, are primarily groups of tools that assist in examining or altering the arrangement of files as needed. They fill gaps in the abilities of DOS and frequently provide a friendlier interface.

While several entirely new functions are provided in these programs, many of their functions are merely faster versions of DOS methods and require fewer and simpler commands. There is also straight duplication of several DOS functions; the DOS methods may be perfectly adequate, but the enhanced user interface makes it worth implementing them from the utility program rather than from the DOS prompt.

The features that directly address the problems described previously will be discussed in this section. Some of these utilities also include features that are indirectly related; these features are mentioned only in reviews of specific programs.

View or Change File Attributes

All these utilities provide access to file attributes beyond the access provided by DOS. Attribute access remains restricted to the attributes of directory entries for files, as opposed to directory entries for volume label or subdirectories. As mentioned previously, file attributes are as follows:

- read-only
- hidden
- system
- archive

Utility programs will usually display hidden files like any other files in a directory listing. Other file operations will remain restricted so the protection provided by the hidden file attribute is not overridden.

The utilities discussed in this book will display the attributes of any file or group of files, which is useful for determining which files are on your disk and the level of access you have to the files.

Equally important, the utilities provide the ability to change file attributes—to read-only, from hidden to nonhidden, and so on. With this facility, you can add protection to files you create and remove attributes that encumber your operations.

Changing a file attribute can be especially useful when, for example, you try to remove a copy-protected application program from a disk. Frequently, copy-protected programs store the protection mechanism in a hidden file.

Suppose you install the program in its own subdirectory and later want to remove the entire application and subdirectory from your disk. Recall that a subdirectory cannot be removed until all files in it have been deleted. The DOS commands DEL and ERASE, however, will not delete hidden files. With these utilities, you can remove the hidden file attribute and delete the file.

Search for a File Across Directories

While subdirectories have many useful characteristics, their existence makes some operations more difficult. If, for example, you don't know which directory contains a file you need, DOS forces you to search each directory separately.

These utility programs, on the other hand, each provide a method to search across subdirectories. All files in any directory on a disk that match a given file name or file name specification with wildcard characters will be simultaneously reported.

Locate a File Containing Specific Text

As mentioned previously, DOS provides the FIND command to locate a given string of text in a file or list of files; however, you must provide the file name specification. Wildcard characters are not allowed; the directory must be explicitly stated.

In contrast, some file management utilities will, in one operation, search all files in any directory for the same text string. While the DOS FIND command searches for the text in a given file, other utilities search for the file containing the text.

View a File's Contents

All file management utilities provide a facility for viewing the contents of a selected file "on the fly." Suppose, for example, you want to give more meaningful names to a group of document files named LETTER1, LETTER2, LETTER3, and so on.

With the View feature, you may quickly view the contents of each file to find the information you need. Because you view these files "on the fly," you don't lose your place or selections in the directory listing.

The utilities provide a display choice of ASCII, hexadecimal, and, frequently, a split-screen option with both types of display. Some utilities also allow you to modify the contents of the file from the View mode.

Move a File Between Directories

Recall that DOS requires two steps to move a file from one directory to another. First, the file must be copied from the original directory to a destination directory. Then the original file must be deleted separately.

Several file management utilities provide a one-step Move operation. Recall that the file's physical starting location is noted in the directory. The physical location of the file, however, does not correspond to the directory in which the file is listed.

The Move operation is accomplished by modifying the source and destination directories without disturbing the file itself. A file entry is added to the destination directory and deleted from the source directory. The file remains in its original physical location.

The method used by the utilities is preferable to the two-step Copy and Delete operation for the following reasons:

- There are fewer user steps.

- The operation is faster because no new space must be found and allocated, and the file contents are not rewritten.

- The operation is safer because the Copy command (which can overwrite any file of the same name without warning) is never used, and the original file is never deleted.

One limitation to the one-step method is that since the file itself does not actually move, the source directory and the destination directory must reside on the same disk.

Sort Directory Entries

The file management utilities outlined in this book improve on the DOS method of sorting a directory display. Each utility provides a simple method of choosing among the following Sort orders:

- file name
- file extension
- file size
- date and time

Most programs allow you to view the files in ascending or descending order for any of these Sort fields.

These improvements primarily make procedures easier to use rather than provide additional functions; however, one outstanding functional improvement offered by each of these programs is the ability to sort by actual, chronological time and date. The utilities use calendar arithmetic rather than the straight ASCII order used by DOS.

Note that in most cases (including the case of the DOS SORT command), changes to the Sort order affect only the current directory display. The Sort feature does not actually reorder the files or the directory. When you exit from the utility program, the directory display remains the same as it was before the Sort operation.

Only a few of the programs in this chapter offer an option to make the new order a permanent change to the directory. See Chapter 1 for other utility programs that offer a similar feature. Be aware, however, that such a change has no impact on the order of future directory entries. New entries will appear in the next available space in the directory.

Rename a Directory

Recall that DOS offers no simple way to change subdirectory names. The effect of renaming a subdirectory may be achieved with DOS commands in four steps, some of which are quite time-consuming:

- MKDIR \new
- COPY \old*.* \new
- DEL \old*.*
- RMDIR \old

File management utilities provide a simple facility for changing subdirectory names. The concept is easy to understand if you recall that a subdirectory is very much like any other computer file; it merely contains the directory entries for the files belonging to the subdirectory.

The one-step procedure requires no creation or removal of directories and no file copying. Utility programs simply access the subdirectory entry and replace the old name with the new name in much the same way that the DOS RENAME command changes any other file name. The subdirectory's contents are not disturbed.

Be cautious when renaming a directory (or a file.) Make sure that any batch files, application programs, or Path statements are updated if they refer specifically to the directory (or file) name.

Remove a Directory

The two-step procedure for removing a subdirectory, i.e., deleting all of the files and then deleting the subdirectory, is used by most of these file management utilities because of safety; you do not inadvertently lose access to files you might still need. Recall from Chapter 1 that "unerasing" a file with utilities is much more difficult if the subdirectory has already been removed, although a few utilities can unerase a subdirectory if you must attempt to unerase one of its files.

Some utilities offer a separate feature to simultaneously perform the two steps. In such cases, one command deletes all files in a subdirectory and then deletes the subdirectory.

View Directories

File management utilities shine in the areas of selection and visual display, which, in addition to cosmetic appearance, provide important functional benefits:

- scrolling back and forth
- displaying additional information
- viewing more than one directory at a time
- selecting files to be included in an operation

Utility programs, unlike DOS, allow you to scroll a directory listing. You may use the cursor keys to move one file at a time and use the Home, End, PgUp, and PgDn keys to move back and forth in the listing. The currently selected file is highlighted.

Any given directory listing remains available for viewing and scrolling until you request a different listing; therefore, you can instantly see the results of your file selections and operations.

Most of these programs also offer a choice of display modes, which affects the number of files that can fit on the screen and the type of information displayed for each file.

Recall that you may use the /w parameter with the DOS DIR command, which expands the number of files displayed but limits the information. File management utilities offer more options with more information, but the same principle applies: the more information displayed, the fewer files appear on the screen at one time.

The additional information that can be displayed by a utility program is available from the directory entry and includes the following:

- file attributes
- disk location of a file's starting cluster
- bytes used by a group of files

The programs described in this chapter offer one or a combination of these items.

Additionally, utilities often provide an option to display files in all directories simultaneously, which is particularly useful when you are looking for files that match a given criterion.

Select a Group of Files

File selection is an outstanding feature of file management utilities. In conjunction with the standard file name specification available with DOS, utility programs also provide for individual and group file selection by other criteria.

The file name specification usually determines which files are displayed; however, a pointer or highlight will mark the displayed files as "selected."

This feature is useful not only for visually analyzing matching file entries but also for performing multiple file operations such as copying, deleting, or moving files to another subdirectory.

Some file management programs allow selection by file attribute. For example, you may select all read-only archive files. Other programs mark hidden files or display all file attributes by default.

Individual and range file selection is provided for complete flexibility in group file designation. Range file selection is particularly useful when files are sorted in a certain order. For example, if the files are sorted by date, it is easy to select all files created after a given date.

Different matching criteria can be used simultaneously to operate on a group of files. For example, you may

- enter the file name specification *.COM to restrict the directory display to machine language program files

- mark all hidden files to select the hidden COM files

- individually select hidden files to be excluded from the group

- individually mark additional selected files to be included in the group

In addition to addressing specific limitations of DOS in this manner, most file management utilities provide features identical to routine DOS file management functions such as COPY, DEL (ERASE), and RENAME.

Utility programs can be used to manage files on floppy diskettes as well as hard disks. You can switch from one drive to another without leaving the program. Through the use of "windows," some programs allow the simultaneous display of directories on different drives.

Most utility programs run at optimal speed when installed as fully RAM-resident. Some provide the user with an option to select fully resident (to maximize speed), partially resident (to minimize RAM allocation), or nonresident status. These options are provided to make room for memory-intensive applications and to eliminate the potential for conflict with other RAM-resident utilities.

The specific features of each utility program are described in the following section.

1dir+/WONDERPLUS

Bourbaki, Inc.
P.O. Box 2867
Boise, Idaho 83701
Telephone: (208) 342-5849

Software Features

1dir+/WonderPlus excels both as a file management utility and a DOS menu utility. The following description focuses on the file management features of the software. See Chapter 4, "DOS Menu Utilities," for a more detailed description of 1dir+'s DOS menu features.

View or Change a File's Attributes

Two of 1dir+'s directory display options display any of the four file attributes already set. 1dir+'s Utility command allows you to change the read-only, hidden, and archive attributes. The read-only and hidden attributes may be changed in both directions. The archive attribute may only be changed from "on" to "off."

Search for a File Across Directories

1dir+'s Locate command will search an entire disk for files matching a file name specification. The resulting display lists the directories along with the matching files.

Locate a File Containing Specific Text

1dir+ offers no facility for searching the contents of a group of files; however, through the View/Edit command, a search for specific text can be performed on a single file.

View a File's Contents

1dir+ contains a sophisticated View/Edit feature that offers three display types: standard ASCII, "extended" ASCII, and hexadecimal. You may edit in any mode.

Viewing functions include scrolling by word, line, or page, scrolling horizontally for wide lines, and, as previously mentioned, searching for specific text.

Editing functions in the ASCII modes include inserting, deleting, and block operations.

The View/Edit feature also allows you to print a block of text, print the entire file, or create a new file.

Move a File Between Directories

The Move command can be used to move one or more files between directories on the same disk drive without duplicating the files.

The destination may be entered by typing the directory name or "pointing" to the directory on the Directory Map.

Sort Directory Entries

Directories can be sorted by file name, extension, date, or size. The Sort options are available through 1dir+'s Directory Personality screen.

The Sort order may be changed for the current display or "permanently," which refers to 1dir+ only; the DOS directory is not physically changed. The Sort order is associated with the directory, so each directory may be permanently sorted on a different key until a new order is saved.

Rename a Directory

Subdirectories and volume labels may be renamed in the same manner as files: using 1dir+'s Rename command. Simply point to the subdirectory and execute the Rename command.

Remove a Directory

1dir+ provides three different ways to remove a subdirectory. The first two methods, as in DOS, require that all subdirectory files be deleted before the subdirectory can be deleted. The directory may then be removed with the Tree command or through the File Management menu.

The other method deletes all the subdirectory's files and removes the subdirectory in one step. KillSub, in the File Management #2 menu, performs this operation.

View Directories

1dir+ offers several directory display options. Displayed directory information ranges from file name, size, date, time, and attribute (one across) to file name only (four across). The "Global Face" option displays all directories and their files.

The directory display may be scrolled with the cursor keys. You may change directories by pointing to (highlighting) a directory and selecting the Run command.

1dir+ also provides a graphic directory tree display that can also be scrolled. Directory-level operations can be performed on the tree itself.

Select a Group of Files

A single file may be individually "flagged" by highlighting it and pressing

<return>

Additional files may be flagged by using the plus sign (+) key and unflagged by using the minus sign (-) key. An option is also provided to flag all displayed files.

The flags disappear after a file operation, but there is an option to reinstate the previous selection.

Other Features

As mentioned previously, in addition to being a complete file management utility, 1dir+ is also a full-featured DOS menu utility. The user interface can be customized from extreme flexibility to precise simplicity.

Extensive on-line help is available, and help screens may be added and tailored to your own needs.

Password security and batch commands may be used to control access to 1dir+'s features so one configuration can accommodate the requirements of different user levels.

The program includes a built-in screen-saver feature to shut off the display if the keyboard is idle for a user-defined period of time.

1dir+ may be run as fully RAM-resident (to maximize speed) or in partially resident (slower, but using one-fifth the amount of RAM) mode. A third option releases all RAM when another application is executed and reloads the program when the application terminates.

THE NORTON COMMANDER/THE NORTON UTILITIES

Peter Norton Computing, Inc.
2210 Wilshire Boulevard, #186
Santa Monica, California 90403
Telephone: (213) 453-2361

Software Features

The Norton Commander is more a DOS menu utility than a file management utility. The Norton Utilities is more a disk maintenance utility than a file management utility. Both of these programs, however, offer considerable file management features.

The following description focuses on each program's file management features. See Chapter 4, "DOS Menu Utilities," for a more detailed description of The Norton Commander's DOS menu features. See Chapter 1 for a detailed description of The Norton Utilities' disk maintenance features.

View or Change a File's Attributes

The Norton Commander can operate on all files, regardless of their attributes. Access to file attributes, however, is limited. Hidden files are marked as such on the directory panel. Cautionary messages are displayed when you operate on a read-only file. File attributes cannot be changed through this program.

The Norton Utilities provides fuller access to file attributes. The four file attributes — read-only, archive, system, and hidden — may be viewed and/or changed with the FA command.

The FA command will operate on individual files or groups of files, which may be defined by file name specification. The file listing may be further limited by an option that confines the display to files with positive attributes. Another option displays only a summary of the number of files with each attribute.

Search for a File Across Directories

The Norton Utilities File Find (FF) command can search an entire disk for files matching a file name specification. The resulting display lists directories and matching files.

The Norton Commander offers a Speed Key feature that performs a similar function. Pressing the Alt key and typing a file name specification scrolls the directory panel to the first matching file or subdirectory within the current directory.

Locate a File Containing Specific Text

The Norton Utilities Text Search (TS) command can search an entire disk, with or without regard to file allocation, for data matching a given string of text. Searching through files is useful for finding a specific file if you recall the subject matter but not the file name. Searching the entire disk is useful for locating and recovering lost data.

You are given an option to receive a summary display of file names in which the matching text appears or to view each occurrence in its context.

The Norton Commander provides no facility for searching the contents of a group of files; however, through the View and Edit commands, you can perform a search for specific text on a single file.

View a File's Contents

Both Norton packages provide features for viewing the contents of files. With The Norton Utilities, you can view any segment of a disk in any of several formats, including standard ASCII, hexadecimal, both ASCII and hexadecimal in side-by-side panels, and EBCDIC. You may edit the data in ASCII or hexadecimal format.

The Norton Commander's View and Edit commands allow you to examine and edit files. These commands are most useful when used as a text editor for straight ASCII files; however, an additional feature displays the ASCII equivalent of any character so non-ASCII data or program files may be examined.

Viewing functions include scrolling back and forth by word, line, or page, scrolling horizontally for wide lines, and searching for specific text.

Editing functions in the ASCII modes include inserting and deleting. The Edit feature also allows you to create a new file.

Move a File Between Directories

The Norton Commander's Rename/Move command can be used to move one or more files without duplication from one directory to another on the same disk drive.

Sort Directory Entries

The Directory Sorting feature, which sorts by file name, extension, date, or size, performs a distinct function in each of these utilities.

In The Norton Commander, the sorting order may be changed for the current directory panel display. This feature makes no physical change to the directory on the disk. The sorting order in the Setup file remains until you change it to automatically incorporate directory modifications.

In The Norton Utilities, however, the DS command physically rearranges a directory on your disk. In this program, you may specify any combination of sort keys, so that files may, for example, be sorted by extension and file name within each group of files with the same extension. This type of sort may be performed in ascending or descending order.

Rename a Directory

The Norton Commander's Rename/Move command can also be used to rename a subdirectory.

Remove a Directory

The Norton Commander Delete command can be used to remove an empty subdirectory. Like DOS, the command requires that all of the subdirectory's files first be deleted. If you attempt to delete a directory that is not empty, DOS displays an error message. No method is provided to delete files and remove a directory in a single step.

View Directories

The Norton Commander offers two directory display options. Displayed directory information may be file name, hidden file indicator, size, date, and time (one across) or file name only (three across). Two different directories may be viewed simultaneously by use of the two display panels.

The directory display may be vertically scrolled with the cursor keys. You may change directories by highlighting a directory and pressing the Return key.

The Norton Utilities List Directories (LD) command generates a file list or summary of directory statistics. The output may include, at your option, all files in all directories or all disk drives. Similar to the DOS TREE and DIR commands, this list may not be scrolled but may be redirected to a file or printer.

Select a Group of Files

With The Norton Commander, a single file can be selected by highlighting it and pressing the Return key. Additional files can be selected or "unselected" by using the Insert key as a toggle. There is also an option to select files by file name specification.

Other Features

As mentioned previously, in addition to being a file management utility, The Norton Commander also works as a DOS menu utility in two ways. First, any executable file can be executed from the directory panel by "pointing and shooting," i.e., highlighting the file name and pressing the Return key. Second, customized menus can be designed to run from function keys. The Norton Commander is designed to allow full control by a mouse.

Also, The Norton Utilities, in addition to being a file management utility, performs many disk maintenance functions. Other features include an on-screen clock and timer and a program to control the tone of the computer's speaker.

Neither program is RAM-resident in the usual sense. Other applications can be run from within The Norton Commander. The program may be operated in one of two modes. The first mode maintains the entire program in RAM while other applications are run. The second mode releases all RAM when another application is executed and reloads the program when the application terminates.

On-line help is available for both utilities.

XTREE

Executive Systems, Inc.
15300 Ventura Boulevard, Suite 305
Sherman Oaks, California 91403
Telephone: (818) 990-3457

Software Features

View or Change a File's Attributes

XTREE directory display options include a display of any of the four file attribute settings. In addition, there is an option to "tag" all files matching a given combination of attributes.

XTREE's Attribute command allows you to turn on or off the read-only, hidden, system, and archive attributes on a single file or group of files.

Search for a File Across Directories

XTREE's ShowAll command displays all files, in all directories, that match a given file name specification. All of these files are then available for other XTREE operations.

Locate a File Containing Specific Text

XTREE provides no facility for searching the contents of a group of files or searching for specific text within a single file; however, with the View command, you may set as many as ten markers in a file being viewed, and you may "jump" to any given marker.

View a File's Contents

XTREE has a View feature that offers two types of display: ASCII and hexadecimal. No editing capability is offered.

Viewing functions include vertical scrolling with the cursor keys and the PgUp, PgDn, Home, and End keys.

The file menu Print command will print the contents of a single file or a group of files in sequence.

Move a File Between Directories

The Move command can be used to move without duplication a single file or group of files from one directory to another on the same disk drive.

Sort Directory Entries

Directories may be sorted by file name, extension, date, or size. The default sorting order is alphabetical by file name.

As long as you are in XTREE, all subsequent directory displays appear in the specified sort order. The DOS directory is not physically changed.

Rename a Directory

A subdirectory can be renamed with the Rename command when the cursor is in the directory window and the subdirectory is highlighted.

Remove a Directory

The Delete command in the directory window can be used to remove an empty subdirectory. As with DOS, all the subdirectory's files must be deleted before the directory can be removed. There is no option to perform this two-step operation with one command.

View Directories

XTREE offers three display options for file information and two display options for the structure of the display screen. Displayed directory information ranges from file name, size, date, time, and attribute (one across) to file name only (three across).

The screen display structure defaults to three panels consisting of a statistical summary, the file listing, and a graphic representation of the directory tree. Optionally, the file-listing area may be expanded, displacing the directory tree.

You may switch between the options; information is instantaneously updated whenever any operation is performed.

The ShowAll command displays all directories and their files.

The file listing and the tree display can be vertically scrolled with the cursor keys. You may change directories by simply pointing to another directory in the tree panel.

Select a Group of Files

A single file may be "tagged" or untagged individually. Groups of files may be tagged by either of two criteria—file name specification or attribute combination.

The number of tagged files and total bytes occupied is updated instantaneously on the statistics panel.

You may perform, within one directory or across all directories, multiple file operations on all tagged files.

Other Features

XTREE provides noteworthy features for use with the Copy command on multiple files. First, you may choose to be prompted for confirmation each time a file of the same name will be overwritten. Second, you will be prompted to change diskettes when the next file to be copied will not fit on the original diskette. Third, you have an option to copy the existing directory structure as well; directories will be created if necessary, and files will be copied to the same directory path on the target disk that the originals occupy on the source disk.

XTREE is not a RAM-resident utility in the usual sense; however, by using the eXecute command, any program or DOS command can be run without leaving XTREE. There are two options for RAM management when eXecuting other programs. One maintains XTREE completely in RAM and updates the disk directory when you return to XTREE. The other frees 100K of RAM but does not automatically update the disk directory.

On-line help is available at the touch of a function key.

PC TOOLS

Central Point Software, Inc.
9700 SW Capitol Highway, #100
Portland, Oregon 97219
Telephone: (503) 244-5782

Software Features

View or Change a File's Attributes

Both of PC Tools' directory display options include a display of any of
the four file attributes that are set. PC Tools' Attribute command allows you to turn on or off the read-only, hidden, system, and archive attributes of any file.

Search for a File Across Directories

PC Tools' Locate command searches an entire disk for files matching a
file name specification. The resulting display lists the directories and
matching files.

Locate a File Containing Specific Text

PC Tools' Find command can search the contents of a single file, a
group of files, or an entire disk to find a string of information, which
may be in ASCII or hexadecimal format.

Search results are reported as the relative sector where a match is
found. For a search by file, this result will be the number of sectors
from the beginning of the file. For a search of an entire disk, this
result will be the absolute sector number on the disk.

The matching sector or sectors can be viewed to determine the context.
For a search by file, the file name remains on the screen display. For a
search of an entire disk, no file information is reported.

View a File's Contents

PC Tools has a View/Edit feature that simultaneously displays the contents of half a sector in both ASCII and hexadecimal format. You may edit in either format.

Viewing functions include vertical scrolling by character or by screen, changing the sector, or "jumping" to the beginning or end of the file.

Move a File Between Directories

The Move command can be used to move one or more files from one directory to another by copying and deleting the source files in a single step.

Sort Directory Entries

Directories can be sorted by file name, extension, date, or size. The sorting order can be changed for the current display only or saved permanently. If you choose the Update option, the DOS directory is physically changed.

Rename a Directory

Directory Maintenance functions include an option to rename a subdirectory. Simply highlight the subdirectory and execute the Rename command.

Remove a Directory

PC Tools' Directory Maintenance functions include an option to remove a subdirectory. As with DOS, this option requires that all the subdirectory's files be deleted first. The directory may then be deleted by pointing to it on a tree display and selecting the Remove Directory command.

PC Tools also provides a unique feature — Prune and Graft — that allows you to move a subdirectory from one parent to another. The operation is similar to renaming or removing a directory. Highlight the directory to be moved and select "Prune." Then, highlight the new parent and select "Graft."

View Directories

PC Tools offers two directory display options. Displayed directory information can include file name, size, date, time, attributes in words, and starting cluster (one across) or file name, size, date, and attributes in acronyms (two across).

The directory display can be vertically scrolled with the cursor keys. The Scroll Lock key can be used to switch between moving the cursor or moving the file list.

The directory tree display can be scrolled in the same manner as the directory file listing. You can change directories by highlighting a directory on the tree display and pressing the Return key.

Select a Group of Files

Files may be selected individually by highlighting them and pressing the Return key. You have an option to select multiple files by file name specification and to "unselect" all files.

Selected files are numbered in the selected order, which is the order to be used for any file operations performed on these files.

Other Features

Using the Attribute command, you can change the date and time stamp of any file.

PC Tools also provides a number of disk maintenance functions, including undeleting a file or subdirectory, verifying the readability of a file or entire disk, and mapping the disk's file allocation.

The System Info command displays useful hardware information such as available peripheral ports and a comparison of the RAM setting vs. the actual amount of available RAM. This information is otherwise attainable, if at all, only by running a special diagnostics diskette.

PC Tools can be run as RAM-resident (to maximize speed) or nonresident. In RAM-resident mode, you may select the amount of RAM to be set aside for PC Tools. The more RAM allocated, the faster the utility will run. Of course, more allocated RAM results in less memory available for other applications.

On-line help is available.

Other Software in this Category

DISKMATE/G-DIRECT

Pico Publishing
305 Second Street, SE
512 Paramount Building
Cedar Rapids, Iowa 52401
Telephone: (319) 362-6964

DISKETTE MANAGER II

Lassen Software, Inc.
P.O. Box 1190
Chico, California 95927
Telephone: (916) 891-6957

DOS HELPER

MetaWare Incorporated
903 Pacific Avenue, Suite 201
Santa Cruz, California 95060-4429
Telephone: (408) 429-6382

DOS FILE TRANSER/FILE COMMAND II

IBM Personally Developed Software
PO Box 3280
Wallingford, Connecticut 06494-3280
Telephone: (800) 426-7279

FILE MATE

Intersecting Concepts
4573 Heatherglen Court
Moorpark, California 93021
Telephone: (805) 529-5073

CHAPTER 3

PATH UTILITIES

Subdirectories are an essential tool for organizing your computer files, especially on a hard disk. **Paths** are the means of identifying each file's location in the directory structure. Access to each file is gained by addressing its path and file name. You must be able to maneuver in and out of subdirectory paths to take full advantage of today's personal computers.

An understanding of paths begins with an understanding of the concepts of directories and subdirectories. A **directory** is like a table of contents to your computer files. In the directory, each file has a line entry that contains the following information:

- the file name and extension
- the number of bytes of disk space allocated to the file
- the date and time the file was created or last modified
- the file attribute flags (hidden, archive, etc.)
- the disk location for the beginning of that file

There are two types of directories: the **root** or main directory and **subdirectories**. The root directory is automatically created, void of entries, on each disk when the disk is formatted. The root directory is fixed in size and, therefore, can accommodate only a finite number of entries — 112 entries on a 360K diskette and 512 entries or more on a hard disk.

Version 2 of MS-DOS provided users with the capability to create more than one directory per disk, using a hierarchical structure. These additional directories are referred to as subdirectories. This capability allows you to organize your computer files into groups of functionally related files.

The root directory is always the first level or the "trunk" in the hierarchical structure. Subdirectories can be viewed as branches off the root directory, each of which is itself a table of contents for a distinct group of files. Each line entry in the root directory may name a file or a subdirectory. Each subdirectory may in turn contain other subdirectories, just as branches grow off other branches of a tree.

In contrast to the root directory, subdirectories have no fixed size; therefore, one advantage to the availability of subdirectories is that the number of directory entries need not be a factor limiting the number of files on a disk.

The principal advantage of subdirectories, however, is their usefulness in organizing the many files you will accumulate on your hard disk. Typically, you will want each of your software applications' files to reside in a separate directory. If you use each application for diverse projects, you may want to segregate your data files further by maintaining separate directories for each project. A typical "tree" structure may resemble the following:

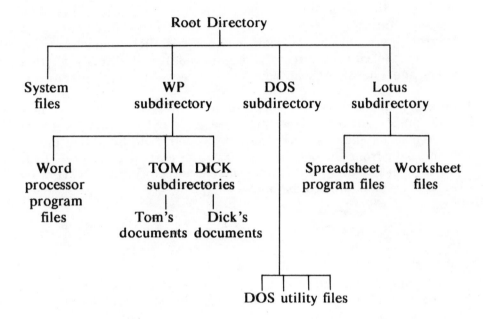

The directory immediately above a particular subdirectory is referred to as the **parent** of the subdirectory. In the example above, the root directory is the parent of the WP, DOS, and Lotus subdirectories. WP is the parent of the TOM and DICK subdirectories.

A file's full identification includes the file name and extension, preceded by the name of the directory in which it is listed, that directory's parent, the parent's parent, and so on until the root directory is reached. This entire identification is called the path.

The root directory is always designated by a backslash (\) at the beginning of the path. Subdirectory names and file names are separated by backslashes within the path. Using the example above, the path to one of Tom's documents is as follows:

`\WP\TOM\filename.ext`

When you first boot your computer, the root directory is the default or "current" directory. You may change the current directory to another directory by means of the DOS CD (or CHDIR) command. Any files listed in the current directory may be addressed directly by their file names and extensions; you may omit the rest of the path identifiers.

Directory names must be specified to address all files listed in directories other than the current one. Files located in lower level subdirectories may be addressed with an abbreviated path, excluding the portion of the path from the root directory to the current directory. From the previous example, if WP is the current directory, one of Tom's documents may be addressed as follows:

`TOM\filename.ext`

In this case, you would not start the path with a backslash. A backslash as the first character in a path always instructs DOS to begin reading from the root directory.

`\TOM\filename.ext`

would result in an error message, since there is no subdirectory named TOM directly below the root directory.

THE PROBLEM

To determine how useful path utility programs may be to you, you must first understand how paths affect your computer operations. All of the files in each of your directories are accessible, but files in different sub-directories are not always accessible simultaneously. There are three principal reasons you may want simultaneous access to files in different subdirectories:

- If you segregate an application's data files by project in different subdirectories, you will need access to the application software and one or more data files at the same time.

- You may want to access one application from within another or one application's data files from another application.

- Novice computer users may not understand the concepts of paths and subdirectories, yet may need to work on more than one application or more than one project within an application (also see Chapter 4, "DOS Menu Utilities").

There are two common barriers to accessing files across subdirectories. First, many software applications, especially older programs written before subdirectories became available, cannot access data files in any directory other than the one in which the program files reside.

Second, application programs frequently consist of more than one file:

- a **control file**, which is called to run the program

- **overlay files**, which the control file loads into RAM as needed

- **text files**, which display messages when help is requested

- a **configuration file**, which defines the program's initial setup parameters

The control file might be addressable from another subdirectory by explicit path identification. But the control file usually expects the related overlay, text, and configuration files to be found in the current directory and may not behave properly if they are not found there.

The DOS PATH command can provide some assistance in the first instance. The PATH command is used to specify one or more directory paths for DOS to search if an executable file is called and not found in the current directory. For example, from the DOS prompt, you might enter the following command:

PATH C:\;C:\DOS

If you call one of the DOS utility programs, such as CHKDSK.COM, from the WP subdirectory, DOS will first search the current directory, then the root directory of the C drive, and, finally, the DOS subdirectory for that program.

However, the DOS PATH command can only search out executable files with file name extensions of .COM, .EXE, or .BAT. Most overlay files have extensions of .OVL. Most text files have extensions such as .TXT, .MSG, .DOC, or .HLP. Most configuration files have different file name extensions. The PATH command will not locate these files.

Rather than foregoing the advantages of structured directories or abandoning otherwise satisfactory software, you may take advantage of one or more practical solutions.

One adequate but imperfect solution is to copy the files and maintain duplicate files in several subdirectories. There are several disadvantages to this approach:

- Redundant files waste precious disk space.

- Updating redundant files wastes precious time and is error-prone.

- New duplicate files must be created each time new subdirectories are created.

- Some copy-protected software may not be able to be copied into more than one directory.

An even better solution is to use a path utility program. The utility programs described in this chapter all work in tandem with the DOS PATH command to make nonexecutable files accessible from any sub-directory.

PATH STRATEGY

Do not expect to install a path utility program on your hard disk, ask it to search every directory each time you call a file, and leave your troubles behind. If you do not plan carefully, you will obtain some un-expected and unwanted results.

There are several factors to keep in mind while planning your strategy:

- The use of subdirectories allows more than one file of the same name to reside on your hard disk. A file name need only be unique within its respective directory.

- The order in which the paths are searched may make a difference as to which file is "found." The current directory is always searched first, followed by the search paths in the order specified.

- New files are always created in the current directory unless explicit paths are designated on the command line that creates the file.

- Different programs and applications will have different path requirements.

- Hidden files have paths like all other files even though they are not displayed in a directory listing.

Also, keep in mind that you may not be aware of various file operations that may be performed by DOS or by your application software, which are affected by paths. Some of these operations are as follows:

- **READ.** Many files are opened for the purpose of reading only. Most program files are only read in the course of normal computer operations. You want to be sure the correct file is read.

- **WRITE** (create or modify). Many file operations involve modifying or creating files even though the user may not explicitly give this instruction. Many applications will create a file if you issue instructions to modify a file not found. Similarly, applications may modify an existing file if you issue instructions to create a file when a file by that name already exists.

- **IF EXIST** (reading the directory). Some programs test for the existence of a file to determine which branch to take.

- **DELETE** or **RENAME.** You or your programs may create temporary files that are later deleted, may rename existing files before creating new files with the original names, or move files between directories by copying to the new directory and then deleting from the original directory.

- **EXECUTE** (run one program from within another program). Some applications provide the ability to run other .EXE or .COM programs without leaving the application. Depending on how the application calls the external program, the DOS PATH command may or may not provide access to a program on a different subdirectory.

The first rule in planning your path strategy is to be consistent. The trick is to be sure that you are always calling the exact file, not another with the same name, for any given application.

Most problems will occur when you modify a file from one directory and read or update it from another directory. If you run a program one time invoking path assistance and another time without path assistance, you may run into trouble.

The best way to ensure consistency is to plan a path strategy that works, incorporate it into a batch file that will run your application, and always run your application from the batch file.

The second rule in planning your path strategy is that less is more. The simplest way you can accomplish your goal is the safest way. Provide access only to the directories you will need. Turn on only those features of the path utility that you will need. If you are not sure, test your application with one feature at a time so that you gain an understanding of the impact of each feature.

A corollary to this rule is to plan the solution to one access problem at a time. If only one application needs path access to only one other subdirectory, write a batch file that invokes that precise access and then runs the application. The batch file should also turn off the path assistance automatically on exiting the application.

The third rule is to try using path assistance to access your program files from the directory containing your data files before you try using it the other way around. First, use the DOS PATH command for executable files. Then use a path utility for overlay, message, and configuration files associated with the executable files. Use path assistance to gain access to your data files only if your goal cannot be fully accomplished using the first two steps.

Finally, before implementing a path strategy, clean up your hard disk of extraneous backup and outdated files with similar or identical names to files on other directories. Delete redundant program files that become unnecessary when you use a path utility.

If you want to keep more than one version of a program file, you may still require some duplication of files; however, you may find you can maintain differently configured versions of an application without duplicating every file in the program. For example, you can install different configurations of Wordstar by maintaining more than one WS.COM file (under different names). Each of these files can share the associated overlay and message files so they do not have to be duplicated.

If you determine that you are going to need path assistance for a specific application, try to organize the data files by project in subdirectories separate from the program files and separate from each other. In this way, each use of the application can be based in a data file directory, giving access only to the specific project's data files and to the program.

THE UTILITIES

The programs described in this chapter provide various levels of file access across directories. They work by intercepting the DOS call to open a file. Opening a file is a different computer operation than running an executable program file. The utility programs can limit their application to nonexecutable files only. They all work in conjunction with the DOS PATH command, which applies to executable files only. The type of access allowed varies with the utility.

Read Access

All of these utility programs allow read access across specified search paths. Reading (or opening) files is the safest operation, since no change is made to the file that is being read; however, other data files may be modified, depending on the information that is read.

For example, suppose you have installed a new version of an application program in a new subdirectory but have kept the original version in its own subdirectory in order to work with older files without converting them. If you inadvertently access the wrong version, the wrong data files may be updated or the right data files may be updated with the wrong information.

Another example is keeping two differently configured versions of a word processing program in separate subdirectories. One version is used for writing programs and is, therefore, configured to produce straight ASCII files unless otherwise instructed. The second version is used for correspondence and is configured to include all document control codes by default. If you inadvertently modify a program file with the wrong version, your program file will be ruined.

Write Access

Directly creating or modifying files involves more obvious planning considerations. Generally, you will know in precisely which subdirectory you want the new or modified file to reside; however, with write access, you can end up with different results, depending on whether or not the file previously existed.

For example, suppose you are using a word processor to modify a document file that resides in a different subdirectory than the word processing program. And suppose you are in the word processing program subdirectory, and you access the document file using path assistance rather than explicitly specifying the path in the file identification.

If your path utility does not assist in writing files, the edited document will be written to the program's subdirectory as a new file. The original document file will not be updated. If your path utility does assist in writing files, no new file will be created. The original document will be overwritten.

If the utility lacks the write access feature or if that feature is turned off, you may still write files. Without this feature, the subdirectory to which the file will be written will be chosen according to normal DOS rules. Usually this subdirectory will be the current directory.

With this feature, the file will be written over a file of the same name if one exists on the search path. If a file of the same name does not already exist anywhere on the search path, a new file will be created in the subdirectory chosen according to normal DOS rules.

Only one of the path utilities reviewed here, File Facility, has the ability to assist in writing files. That option may be turned off or on.

Reading Directories

Path utilities do not usually define the directories read by the DOS DIR function. Of the utilities reviewed here, Filepath is the only one that has an option allowing path assistance for the DIR function.

This option also affects the operation of some other DOS commands, notably IF EXIST (in a DOS batch file), COPY, and COMP.COM.

Reading a directory or testing for a file's existence may produce misleading results if you are using path assistance. While a file may exist somewhere on the accessible paths, you may not be able to ascertain in which directory it exists.

You should be particularly careful using the DOS COPY command when this option is in effect. For large files, copying a file onto itself could have disastrous consequences. DOS normally tries to protect you from this occurrence by comparing the specified source file name and path with the target file name and path; however, if a file is accessible both with and without a path specification, a COPY will be allowed if the source file is specified by file name only and the target file by file name and path or vice versa.

Conversely, a file may not be copied from a search path to the current directory if no path is specified with either the source or the target file names. In this case, DOS will erroneously believe you are trying to copy the file onto itself.

As a safety measure, utilities that have this option may require you to specify a precise file name without wildcard characters. If wildcard characters (* or ?) are used, the DOS rules will be followed rather than the path utility's search path.

Other DOS Commands

DOS commands that do not open files, such as DELETE or RENAME, are typically not affected by the path utility search paths. None of the utility programs reviewed here affects the search paths for a DELETE or RENAME command.

Running Programs from within Programs

There is one apparent exception to the rule that the DOS PATH command can access any executable file, and the file utilities cannot access any executable file. Some applications allow you to run external .EXE or .COM programs from within the application. If this feature is implemented by use of the DOS execute function, the DOS PATH command is not used to search for the file. In these cases, you must specify the path to the external program, or the external program must be in the current directory.

For example, suppose Wordstar resides in a directory named WS, and CHKDSK.COM resides in a directory named DOS. Suppose further that the DOS PATH is \DOS, and your current directory is WS. If you want to run CHKDSK.COM from within Wordstar, you can select "R" from Wordstar's main menu to execute (or run) a program with an .EXE or .COM extension.

You are then asked to enter the name of the program to run. Wordstar version 3.3, written before subdirectories became available, does not recognize path indicators entered with file names; however, if you enter CHKDSK without a path indicator, an error message will be returned because the file will not be found.

In this case only, these path utility programs do provide access to the executable files. If \DOS is one of the search paths specified by the path utility, CHKDSK.COM will be found and run.

Each of the path utilities reviewed here performs this function. Most path utilities will do so as long as the utility is activated. Filepath, however, is unique among the utility programs reviewed here in that it allows you to switch this particular feature off independently of the other functions.

Installation

All of the path utilities reviewed here are RAM resident, meaning that once invoked, they remain present in your computer's internal memory while other programs are run. These programs take up minimal space in RAM —each under 3,000 bytes —so using up RAM space is not a major consideration.

As with any RAM-resident utility, you should be careful of potential conflicts with other RAM-resident utilities. Each of the utilities interacts with DOS in a slightly different way.

Filepath is installed as a DOS device driver. Since device drivers are loaded into a separate part of memory, distinct from the chain of most RAM-resident utilities, the potential for conflict with other utilities is minimized.

Smartpath and File Facility are more typical RAM-resident programs. They will intercept the appropriate DOS functions if another resident program does not intercept them first.

Some utilities also make use of a special section of memory called the DOS **environment**. The environment contains, among other things, the most recent path specification. In File Facility, for example, an alternative search path can be added to the environment. The only potential problem with this mode of operation is that the environment size is limited. If you run out of environment space, you may need to delete some environment parameters.

Turning Off the Search Path

Like most resident utilities, these programs cannot be unloaded once they have been loaded, except by rebooting your computer.

Each of these programs has provided another way for you to disable them when they are not required for your operations. You can disable the utility program by simply setting all of the search options off.

Alternatively, you may want to bypass the search paths for just one command line. For example, you may want to address a particular file for one operation by its specific path identifier in order to eliminate any potential for conflict. Each of these utilities will accept an explicit file identification if full paths are included in the file specification. The path you indicate overrides the utility's search path.

Selectivity

Each of these utility programs allows you to specify search paths independently of the DOS PATH command. The search paths for the executable files may, therefore, differ from the search paths for nonexecutable files.

Generally, the search path is entered using the same kind of notation required by the DOS PATH command. Drive designators may be entered to specify a search path on a drive other than the default drive. Multiple search paths may be entered, separated by semicolons. Wildcard characters may be used in file names.

Some path utilities add the following types of flexibility to the parameters allowed:

- allow wildcard characters in directory names as well as file names

- provide the option to automatically include all lower level subdirectories of a given directory

User Interface

Most of these path utilities are accessed by entering a command line from the DOS prompt. The command line syntax is usually very similar to the DOS PATH command syntax. The difference is in the optional parameters that are specified after the paths in the command line.

You can call the utilities repeatedly, each time entering only the parameter you want to change. Remember, however, that as long as the utility is loaded, the parameters remain until explicitly changed.

The command line can always be placed in a DOS batch file. Some utility programs also provide a facility for saving the parameters to a set-up file. Once you settle on your path strategy, you can activate a utility automatically through the use of batch and setup files. Be aware, however, that the utility program must be accessible to the batch file prior to running the batch file.

Some utilities also offer a menu interface. This type of interface can ease the entry of search path specifications and options. The default, or previously set, path specifications and options are displayed on the screen. You then use the cursor keys to move to the section you want to change and enter the changes.

Following are descriptions of the specific features of each utility program.

FILE FACILITY

IBM Personally Developed Software
PO Box 3280
Wallingford, Connecticut 06494-3280
Telephone: (800) 426-7279

Software Features

Read Access

The default setting for File Facility enables the function that reads or "opens" files. This setting may be turned off by entering /NO (for no open) at the command line. The setting may be turned back on by entering /O at the command line.

As long as the open function is enabled, any file called will be searched for along the paths specified.

Write Access

File Facility is the only path utility reviewed here that allows write or "create" access. The default setting for File Facility disables this function. The setting may be turned on by entering /C at the command line. It may be turned back off by entering /NC at the command line.

When this feature is enabled, a file that is modified or created will be written over a file of the same name if one exists on the search path. If a file of the same name does not already exist anywhere on the search path, a new file will be created in the subdirectory chosen according to normal DOS rules.

Read access may be enabled while write access is disabled; however, the reverse is not true. If conflicting options are given on the same command line, the options are processed from left to right so the last option has precedence. Entering /C enables both read and write access. Entering /NO disables both read and write access.

Reading Directories

File Facility does not affect the DOS DIR function. The DIR command, and other commands such as RENAME and COPY, will not search the designated search paths. If no path is designated in the file specification, the current directory is assumed.

These operations may still be performed on files in directories other than the current directory by explicitly including the correct path in the file specification.

Running Programs from within Programs

If an application uses the DOS execute function to run an external program without exiting the application, File Facility can find the external program. File Facility can find an executable file in this situation if it exists on the designated search path and read access is enabled.

Installation

FILE FACILITY is a RAM-resident utility. The program is loaded into RAM initially by entering

```
FILEFAC /I
```

from the DOS prompt. Options may be selected on the initial command line. File Facility then remains in RAM until you reboot your computer.

File Facility also makes use of the DOS **environment**. An alternative search path for File Facility can be added to the environment, using the DOS SET command. When you instruct File Facility to reset its search path, the program will look up the environment for the alternative path. If no alternative path is found, the DOS path is used.

Environment space is limited. If you want separate long paths for DOS and for File Facility, you may conserve environment space by following these steps:

- Set the path in the environment.

- Instruct File Facility to reset its path from the environment.

- Delete the path from the environment.

- Set the DOS path.

Turning Off the Search Path

FILE FACILITY search paths may be disabled by entering

```
FILEFAC /NO
```

from the DOS prompt. The specified search paths remain active, but no read or other operations will search those paths.

Alternatively, if you want to bypass the search paths for just one command line, simply address the file by its explicit path. File Facility will interpret literally any call to a file whose file specification begins with a backslash.

Selectivity

The search path is entered using the same kind of notation required by the DOS PATH command. If no search path is specified, File Facility adopts the DOS path by default.

A File Facility search path different from DOS can be specified by
entering

SET FF=search path

from the DOS prompt to store the alternative path in the DOS environment. Then enter

FILEFAC /P

also from the DOS prompt to instruct File Facility to read the search path from the environment.

File Facility has a unique approach to situations in which a program includes an explicit drive specification in a file address. This situation is often found in programs written before hard disks became popular. File Facility first tries to find the file on the drive specified, usually a floppy disk drive. If the file is not found or no diskette is in the drive, File Facility then searches for the file in the current directory and the search path as if no drive had been specified.

User Interface

File Facility is accessed by entering from the DOS prompt FILEFAC followed by the option selections. The search path is not entered on the same command line that invokes the program.

The command line to set the search path and the command line to invoke the program can always be placed in a DOS batch file.

File Facility includes an option to save the current settings before changing the parameters. An option to restore the saved settings is also provided. This feature is useful if, for example, you want to change the settings to run one application, and then change back to the initial settings when you exit the application.

FILEPATH

SDA Associates
P.O. Box 36152
San Jose, California 95158
Telephone: (408) 281-7747
Modem: (415) 794-9624

Software Features

Read Access

The default setting for Filepath enables the function that reads or "opens" files. This setting may be turned off by specifing /FO at the command line. The setting may be turned back on by specifying /FI at the command line.

As long as the open function is enabled, any file called will be searched for along the paths specified.

Write Access

Filepath does not assist with writing, creating, or modifying files. You may still write files without path assistance. The subdirectory to which the file will be written will be chosen according to normal DOS rules. Usually this subdirectory will be the current directory.

Filepath is the only utility reviewed here that has an option that allows path assistance for the DIR function. This option is selected by including /DI in the command line. The DIR option is disabled by entering /DO in the command line. The default setting is /DO.

This option is only recommended for applications that cannot otherwise find files in certain operations. Early versions of MultiMate, for example, will not be able to locate dictionary files without this option.

The DOS commands DIR, COPY, COMP, and IF EXIST (in batch files) are all affected by this option. The Filepath search paths will be followed if you use these commands with the DIR option enabled *and* precise file names without wildcard characters are specified.

If wildcard characters (* or ?) are used, the DOS rules will be followed rather than the path utility's search path.

Running Programs from within Programs

If an application uses the DOS execute function to run an external program without exiting the application, Filepath can find the external program. Filepath can find an executable file in this situation if it exists on the designated search path and read access is enabled.

Filepath, however, is unique among the utility programs reviewed here in that it allows you to switch this particular feature off independently of the other functions. This option is selected by including /EI in the command line. The EXEC option is disabled by entering /EO in the command line. The default setting is /EO.

Installation

Filepath is installed as a DOS device driver. Since device drivers are loaded into a separate part of memory, distinct from the chain of most RAM-resident utilities, the potential for conflict with other utilities is minimized.

The CONFIG.SYS file must be modified to include FPSYS.COM as a device driver. The CONFIG.SYS file always resides in the root directory; therefore, either the FPSYS.COM file must also reside in the root directory, or the CONFIG.SYS file must address that file by its explicit path.

Turning Off the Search Path

Filepath search paths may be disabled by entering

```
FP  /F0
```

from the DOS prompt. The specified search paths remain active, but no read or other operations will search those paths.

Alternatively, if you want to bypass the search paths for just one command line, simply address the file by its explicit path. Filepath will interpret literally any call to a file whose file specification begins with a backslash.

Selectivity

Filepath is also the only path utility reviewed here that adds flexibility to the path specification parameters allowed. When specifying the search path, wildcard characters are allowed in directory names in the same way they are used in file names.

In addition, Filepath provides a **tree** option. If /T is entered on the command line immediately after a search path, the search path automatically includes all subdirectories of the defined directories, all of their subdirectories, and so on. These implicit subdirectories are searched in the order presented by DOS.

Filepath provides a type of menu interface in its Screen Editor Option. The screen editor is invoked by entering

FP ED

from the DOS prompt. The current file search specifications and options are displayed on the screen. You then use the cursor keys to move to the section you want to change and enter the changes.

Filepath can also be accessed by entering from the DOS prompt FP followed by the option selections. The search path can be entered on the same command line that invokes the program. The command line may be placed in a DOS batch file.

File Facility includes an option to save the current settings on a command line to a setup file or restore settings from a previously saved setup file. This procedure is accomplished by using the redirection symbols (> to save and < to restore), followed by the setup file name, on the command line.

SMARTPATH

Software Research Technologies
3757 Wilshire Boulevard, Suite 211
Los Angeles, California 90010
Telephone: (213) 384-5430

Software Features

Read Access

The default setting for Smartpath enables the function that reads or "opens" files. This setting may be turned off by specifing /OFF in the command line. The setting may be turned back on by specifying /ON in the command line.

As long as the Open function is enabled, called files will be searched for along specified paths.

Write Access

Smartpath does not assist with writing, creating, or modifying files. You may still write files without path assistance. The subdirectory to which the file will be written will be chosen according to normal DOS rules. Usually this subdirectory will be the current directory.

Reading Directories

Smartpath does not affect the the DOS DIR function. The DIR command, and other commands such as RENAME and COPY, will not search the designated search paths. If no path is designated in the file specification, the current directory is assumed.

These operations may still be performed on files in directories other than the current directory by explicitly including the correct path in the file specification.

Running Programs from within Programs

If an application uses the DOS Execute function to run an external program without exiting the application, Smartpath can find the external program. Smartpath can find an executable file in this situation if it exists on the designated search path and read access is enabled.

Installation

Smartpath is a RAM-resident utility. The program is loaded into RAM initially by entering

```
SPATH search path
```

from the DOS prompt. There are no options to select. Smartpath then remains in RAM until you reboot your computer.

Smartpath search paths may be disabled by entering

SPATH /OFF

from the DOS prompt. The specified search paths remain active, but no read or write operations will search those paths.

Alternatively, if you want to bypass the search paths for just one command line, simply address the file by its explicit path. Smartpath will interpret literally any call to a file that includes a backslash in the file specification.

Selectivity

The search path is entered, using precisely the same syntax required by the DOS PATH command.

Entering SPATH without a search path will display the current search path.

User Interface

In all of these areas, Smartpath is the simplest of the path utilities reviewed here. While it offers the fewest options, it is the least complex and the easiest to learn.

Smartpath is accessed by entering SPATH followed by the search path from the DOS prompt.

The command line may be placed in a DOS batch file.

Other Software in this Category

PATHMINDER

Westlake Data Corp.
505 West 15th
Austin, Texas 78701
Telephone: (512) 474-4666

DPATH-PLUS

Personal Business Solutions, Inc.
PO Box 739
Frederick, Maryland 2701
Telephone: (301) 865-3376

CHAPTER 4

DOS MENU UTILITIES

The disk operating system — PC-DOS or MS-DOS — is the primary connection between you and the computer. You may use DOS's own powerful language to perform a wide range of tasks. Like many computer languages, DOS may be operated on two levels: **command** and **program**.

At the command level, an experienced DOS user enters instructions directly from the keyboard. DOS translates the instructions into machine language and performs them immediately. DOS is capable of performing extremely complex tasks.

Alternatively, DOS may be programmed with lists of instructions to be performed sequentially at another time. The instructions are translated and executed when you "run" the program. Once programmed, complex tasks may be accomplished with very few keystrokes. A program is useful for two reasons:

- it minimizes the input required for repetitive tasks

- it simplifies the procedure for less knowledgeable users

At the command level, like most operating systems and computer languages, DOS is *not* "user-friendly"; it must be learned before it can be effectively used. This limitation is not always a disadvantage; user-friendliness is generally accompanied by less flexibility and slower operation.

Most computer users, however, don't need to master DOS to perform daily tasks; simple access to application programs and a few DOS commands can support most routine work.

DOS menu utilities provide a friendlier DOS interface. Executing the most common DOS commands becomes much simpler and self-evident. Also, these utilities are easily tailored to simplify the execution of application programs.

The DOS menu utilities discussed in this book can work with floppy diskettes as well as hard disks, but hard disk users receive greater benefits because more application programs can be simultaneously present in their computer's memory.

Read the respective chapters on "Keyboard Enhancers" and "Windows." Many functions performed by keyboard enhancers and window utilities serve similar purposes as DOS menus, and vice versa.

THE PROBLEM

The typical personal computer monitor displays 25 lines of text, each 80 characters wide. When you first "boot" your computer with DOS, you are presented with a screen similar to the following:

```
Current Date is Tue  1-01-1980
Enter New Date (MM-DD-YY):

Current Time is 0:00:47.45
Enter New Time:

A>__
```

You are first asked, in reasonably plain English, to enter the time and date. Then a letter —usually A or C—appears followed by a greater-than (>) sign, which is followed by a blinking line.

The nearly blank screen offers no clue as to what you should do next. If you attempt to guess what to enter from the keyboard, you will probably end up with unwanted results.

For example, if you press the Return key a few times, you will see the following results:

```
A >
A >
A >
A > __
```

If you type in a random word and press the Return key, you will see
the following:

```
A > help
bad command or file name

A > __
```

Finally, if you enter a word DOS recognizes but can't process, you will
see the following:

```
A>type
invalid number of parameters

A>__
```

You must read the manual to learn how to communicate with a computer through DOS. DOS, like any language, has its own vocabulary and rules of syntax.

While the vocabulary and syntax of DOS commands are based on the English language, they are far from self-evident; they must be learned. You must memorize the language or look up the commands. Then, you must enter the commands through the keyboard. If you misspell the commands or experience undesired results, you will need to start over.

There are a number of problems with the DOS interface:

- the difficulty of memorizing vocabulary and syntax

- the number of keystrokes required to enter one command

- the number of commands required to accomplish a single routine task

- the difficulty of error-correction while entering commands

- the difficulty of obtaining help

In fact, few computer users memorize the entire DOS vocabulary and syntax. Experienced users often memorize the syntax logic, but there are exceptions to this logic, as with any language. Even experienced users refer to the DOS manual to perform non-routine tasks.

Even if you are familiar with DOS, you might legitimately complain about the number of keystrokes required to enter a routine command. If the command is required frequently, it may seem a waste of time to type the entire command line each time.

DOS provides assistance in entering repetitive commands through the function keys. For example, pressing

[F1]   repeats the previous command line one letter at a time

[F2] x   where x is any letter in the previous command line, repeats the line up to that letter

[F3]   repeats the entire command line

These function keys are only helpful when you need to repeat the preceding line. If you have entered another command since the desired command line, you must reenter the desired command.

Another common complaint concerns the number of command lines required to accomplish a routine task. Each time you run a task, you must reenter an entire sequence of commands. Furthermore, to perform an operation that requires you to enter several command lines, you often must wait until each command line is processed before entering the next line.

A batch file facility is provided by DOS to address this problem. A **batch file** is a text file consisting of DOS command lines to be sequentially executed. A batch file is a DOS program. DOS provides unique commands and parameters relevant only to batch files, including

ECHO/REM   to display a comment line that will not be executed

ECHO OFF   to turn off the display of commands as they are executed

PAUSE   to wait for keyboard input before continuing

%n   a variable to be defined by user input when the batch file is run

IF   to evaluate a condition before proceeding

GOTO   to allow for branching, typically on evaluation of a condition.

Batch files can be created or edited with any text editor or word processor that can produce ASCII files, including the EDLIN program provided with DOS. They may also be created directly from the DOS prompt by using the COPY command.

The COPY command is often used to duplicate a file on a different disk and/or under a different file name; however, any DOS device may serve as the input or the output. A DOS **device** may be a file or a peripheral such as your printer or keyboard. The printer is referred to as PRN; the keyboard is referred to as CON (for console); therefore, if you type

`COPY CON filename.BAT`

at the DOS prompt and press the Return key, subsequent keyboard input will be copied to a file named FILENAME.BAT. This method is a simple way of writing a short batch file. The copying process ends when an end-of-file (Ctrl/z) marker is encountered. Enter such a marker directly from the keyboard by typing ^Z or pressing the <F6> function key.

A batch file is run by typing the name of the file from the DOS prompt and pressing the Return key. When you run a DOS batch file, each command line is executed sequentially as if you entered each command separately from the DOS prompt.

Batch files are helpful, but they do have limitations. You must still type the entire name of the batch file as if the name of your batch file is a DOS command; therefore, you must still memorize your batch file's name. One exception exists; if you create a batch file called AUTOEXEC.BAT in the root directory of the disk you boot from, it will run automatically when you boot your computer.

You can use batch files to create your own menu system. You may write a DOS batch file to display a list of options on your screen — program names and/or DOS commands — in addition to text that tells you what to do to select each of the options.

DOS was not invented with this purpose in mind, so a fair number of command lines in several text files may be required to achieve the menu system you want. One batch file may be called from another, but DOS can keep track of only one batch file at a time. Creating a menu system requires clever manipulation to transfer control between batch files.

All these problems are compounded by the difficulty of error-correction while you enter commands. DOS provides minimal editing capabilities as you enter commands directly from the DOS prompt. You can correct an error in the line you are typing only before pressing the Return key, and the only correction possible is backspacing through (and deleting) characters up to the erroneous one and retyping the remainder of the line.

If you discover an error after you have pressed the Return key, usually after not achieving the desired results, you can use the function keys described above to reenter the line. The Insert and Delete keys can be used in conjunction with the function keys to correct the errors.

The function keys can also be used with the EDLIN text editor; in fact, these features were provided for such a purpose; however, they will not help while you are creating a batch file with the COPY CON command if you discover an error after pressing the Return key. In this case, you must end the file with ^Z or interrupt the command with ^C and then reenter the entire batch file. Batch files are not easy to set up without a text editor.

Finally, if you find these procedures complicated or forget how to perform a given operation, no on-line help is available. DOS provides context-sensitive error messages, but no on-line information or help screens. Your only resources are the manual and other experienced computer users.

On the other hand, someone may have provided your computer with a menu system, usually either a DOS program or commercial utility program. In this case, when you turn on your computer, your screen will display a list of options — program names, tutorials, and/or DOS commands — in addition to text telling you what to do to select each of the options.

DOS MENU STRATEGY

Like many computer programs, menu utilities can be approached on three different levels:

- tailored by experienced users for those with less technical expertise

- used "out of the box" by users with little technical expertise

- used by experienced users to perform routine tasks

The best approach for you depends on the distribution of responsibility in your computing environment. One way of defining a personal computing environment is to classify where it falls between these two extremes:

- The person responsible for setup and maintenance is also the primary user.

- The primary user is not the same person who is responsible for setup and maintenance.

A related factor is the number of users per machine and whether different people are using the same computer for different applications.

If you are setting up a menu system for yourself, your goals are different than if you are setting up a menu system for others. The following issues should be considered:

- simplicity
- on-line help
- password security
- access to DOS
- flexibility

Suppose, for example, that you are employed in a corporate systems department and your task is to bring another department into the computer age. The following conditions exist:

- One computer has been purchased.

- A word processing application will be used primarily by the secretary and occasionally by two other staff members.

- Spreadsheet software is used by the same two staff members.

- Each person needs access to worksheet and document files created by the others.

- The department functions as a training ground, so there tends to be high turnover.

- The employees have neither the time nor the inclination to experiment with other computer programs.

In this case, simplicity and on-line help are important. You must provide access to only two applications: word processing and spreadsheet software. On-line help can be used to avoid lengthy introductory sessions for new employees.

Password security is neither necessary nor desirable. The employees need access to each other's files. A high turnover would require frequent password changes, and access is difficult if password security is used.

On the other hand, there is little need for access to DOS commands. For the most part, data files can be backed up with copying facilities provided by applications. Other DOS commands may be dangerous in the hands of inexperienced users. Required DOS maintenance can be performed by a member of the corporate systems department on either a routine or as-needed basis; therefore, access to DOS should not be available through the menu, or it should be available only with a password known to systems department employees.

Flexibility is neither necessary nor desirable. Systems department employees can be called on for unusual, one-time requirements or permanent changes to routine requirements. Systems department employees can entirely bypass the menu system or gain access to DOS or menu setup modules via the password.

Suppose, in contrast, that you are the only administrative employee in a small, stable business. You do not consider yourself an expert. Every day, you use a word processing program and an accounting application, switching between them several times a day. Data files from the accounting program must be copied monthly to diskettes and carried via messenger to an outside accountant.

In this case, simplicity and on-line help are less important because you know the routine; however, ease and speed of operation are always helpful. The menu program will eliminate the need to enter long, repetitive commands each time you want to enter or exit an application. Password security would be more of a nuisance than help because no other office workers use the computer.

Access to DOS and other flexibility features are important. Although you may know how to disable the menu system, you might make changes and use DOS commands frequently enough to make ease of access desirable.

Once you have analyzed the needs of your computing environment, you must compose specific menus. The purpose of DOS menu utilities is to simplify such tasks. Specific examples in computer books and manuals may illustrate *how* to set up menus; you, however, determine *what* you want to accomplish.

Set up the menus your way. For the average computer user, the primary stumbling block to thorough menu setup is trying to visualize all future requirements in advance. A more successful strategy for this type of utility, on the other hand, is to begin with what you already know you want.

While you may have access to many applications on a hard disk or floppy diskettes, your day-to-day operations probably involve only a few applications. You may use your computer every day for months at a time, accessing only one or two applications and a backup utility program.

If you previously used batch files to access these applications, you may decide to use the menu system to access the batch files or to use the menu system instead of the batch files.

In you intend to replace batch files, examine your batch files carefully before proceeding. This examination will help you recall all the steps routinely executed before entering or after exiting each application. Do not delete the original batch files until testing to see if you have defined the correct procedures in your menu system to achieve the desired results.

Pay close attention to your subdirectory structure. A menu utility may provide a quicker way to enter an application than you previously used with DOS, but if you change the access method, you may also need to find new ways to control the subdirectory in which you end up.

While menu systems can be set up with DOS, the utilities described in the following section expand the options and make the process easier.

THE UTILITIES

DOS menu utilities, for the most part, fall into a category of utilities that achieve results possible with DOS but in an easier and more direct way. Occasionally, new functions are offered with these programs.

Two types of menu utilities are described here:

- those that are called menu utilities
- those that serve several functions of a more general purpose

Helpful features may include

- visual display of options
- minimal keystroke requirements
- screen and command line editing
- support for multiple-menu levels
- ready-made menus and help screens
- password security
- fast execution

Visual Display

All menu utilities described in this chapter provide a visual display of options, which is their primary purpose. Rather than making you guess or go elsewhere for information, all options are presented on the screen. In the area of visual display, there are two principal benefits to menu utilities as compared to DOS-created menus:

- graphic appearance
- display manipulation

Menu utilities each have a carefully designed, predefined format. Some utilities emphasize simplicity with few options and much space on the screen. Others emphasize utility, packing a great deal of information onto the 25-line by 80-character monitor screen.

Graphic characters (such as horizontal and vertical lines and boxes) and graphic emphasis (such as highlighting, boldface lettering, and color) are used freely to enhance the displays. These features are used to make the important functions quickly and easily accessible without causing user eyestrain.

Some of these enhancements can be created with the use of DOS only and some cannot. Even those that can be duplicated, however, require the knowledge of obscure DOS commands and advanced text processing functions.

Regardless of how well a menu is designed, however, there is a limit to the amount of information that can fit on the screen. Menu utilities also make full use of all cursor keys, including Home, End, PgUp, and PgDn. With these facilities, you can quickly peruse a long list or several pages of menus.

Keystroke Requirements

Obviously, a menu decreases the number of keystrokes required to find information. If a list scrolls past the screen, you need not reenter the command.

Display features also contribute to the ease with which menu selections are chosen. With DOS, you have no choice but to enter characters from the keyboard to designate your selection and press the Return key. This method increases the number of keystrokes required, which increases the opportunity for error.

With several menu utilities, you simply move through options with cursor keys and highlight (or point to) the one you want. Then, you need only press one key, usually Return, to execute your choice.

Menu utilities also limit the number of required keystrokes by allowing you to designate a single menu selection to execute a number of commands in sequence. This feature is similar to the creation and use of DOS batch files; however the "batch" of commands is executed more easily by these enhanced methods of selection.

Screen Editing

A menu format is usually provided to help you more easily create the screen display. You don't need to reinvent the design each time a menu is created; just enter two or three elements for each menu option to be displayed, perhaps including

- a short code (often a letter or number) that will be entered or highlighted in the selection process

- a longer description to aid the user in understanding what each option stands for

- the DOS command or sequence of commands to be executed each time the option is selected.

Several of these menu utilities contain limited but sophisticated text processors to simplify the process of creating and editing menus. Some utilities also allow you to create menus with any text processor that can produce straight ASCII files, as long as you follow the required format, which means that you do not need to learn yet another program if your favorite word processor suffices.

A related feature offered by many of these programs is an editor for direct DOS commands. With significantly more flexibility than DOS alone offers, you can compose a DOS command line from within the menu system as if you were entering a command from the DOS prompt.

Multiple-Menu Levels

Some of these utilities support multiple levels of menus. This feature is often provided by utilities with simpler, sparser screen formats. Since the amount of information that can appear on a screen is often limited, multiple-menu levels offer more flexibility.

With multiple levels, each menu selection may execute a sequence of commands, display help information, or bring up a submenu. Submenus, like subdirectories, are usually attached to a single parent.

Ready-Made Menus and Help Screens

Your setup tasks are simplified even more by menu utilities that provide ready-made display screens, which appear in one of two ways:

- pre-created menus of commonly used DOS commands and accompanying help text

- visual display of all accessible executable files in menu format

When ready-made screens provide access to the commonly used DOS commands, you are prompted upon selection for parameters to be used with a command; however, with this facility, you no longer have to memorize the vocabulary or syntax.

Other utilities simply display all files in a directory. You may select to execute any currently accessible, executable machine language or batch file.

Password Security

Password security is offered by several menu utility programs. In some programs, password security can restrict entry to certain options or submenus. In other programs, password security controls menu utility access.

While this feature is easy to implement, note that software passwords do not provide a very high level of security. A user familiar with DOS can easily bypass the menu. On the other hand, since many people will use these utilities specifically because they are not familiar with DOS, this level of protection may be adequate.

Speed of Execution

In computing, speed of operation is as important as ease of operation. The speed at which manually entered commands are executed is at least as long as it takes you to enter the command. In addition, a manually-entered DOS command or a batch file must be translated from ASCII to machine language before it can be executed.

Some utility programs speed up execution by compiling the DOS instructions into machine language each time a selection is created or edited. In this way, execution immediately follows an option's selection.

The speed of the menu system — for example, how fast the menu reappears after an option has been executed — often depends on whether or not it is memory-resident. Memory-resident programs are faster because they need not be reloaded each time you want access to them, but they use up valuable RAM and occasionally cause conflicts with other software. Several of these menu utilities allow you to choose whether the utility stays in RAM totally, partially, or not at all.

The specific features of each utility program are described in the following section.

1dir+/WONDERPLUS

Bourbaki, Inc.
P.O. Box 2867
Boise, Idaho 83701
Telephone: (208) 342-5849

Software Features

1dir+ (WonderPlus) excels as both a file management utility and a sophisticated DOS menu utility. The following description focuses on the menu features of the software. See Chapter 2, "File Management," for a more detailed description of 1dir+'s file management features.

Visual Display of Options

1dir+ offers eight "faces" from which to choose. One face is simply the minimal DOS display. Six of the eight faces display file names with other information such as statistics on directory, disk, and RAM use, additional file statistics, or help information. File names may be scrolled with the cursor keys. Function key options are displayed across the bottom of the screen.

The remaining face, the Menu Only Face, is a less busy display. Function keys are listed vertically in a box on the left side of the screen. For each function key, a line of text displayed in a box on the right side of the screen describes the operation the key will perform. These operations and descriptions are defined as the user sets up the menu system. Help text may be defined to be displayed in pop-up windows overlapping the menu.

Foreground and background colors may be specified for any of these faces.

Minimal Keystroke Requirements

1dir+ utilizes the "point-and-shoot" method of selecting and executing commands. From the file name faces, you can point to any executable file (with a COM, EXE, or BAT extension) using the cursor keys to scroll to the desired program file. Pressing the Return key will run (or execute) the selected program.

From the Menu Only Face, as well as any menu option for the other faces, you can use either of two methods to select an operation. First, you can simply press the corresponding function key. Alternatively, you can use the cursor keys to point to your selection and then press the Return key to execute it.

Screen and Command Line Editing

1dir+ includes several facilities for customizing the menu system. The major facilities are directory personalities, command menus, and the menu-only face. None of these facilities uses text editors in the usual sense; rather, 1dir+ provides templates that may be filled with user specifications.

Directory personalities manage the display and file access in a particular directory. You may limit the files to be displayed by file name specification, attribute, and date and define the order in which the files are sorted. Both a face and a command menu may be specified. You can, for example, specify that on changing to your Lotus 1-2-3 directory, you will see only worksheet files sorted by file name in the extended directory format.

Command menus that appear across the bottom of the file name faces can be customized in two ways. Menus can be created and edited to be run from the already existing Programs option. In addition, all existing menu options may be modified.

The Menu Only face can be set up for users who don't need the more powerful file access provided by the other faces. Selections may be limited to a few applications. Commands are executed in the same way as in any other face, but choices are limited to those displayed on the screen.

Help screens for any 1dir+ command may be created or edited through 1dir+'s text editor.

1dir+ also provides assistance in entering and editing DOS commands. From the File Management submenu, you may "bring down" any file name to the DOS command line, which is a useful shortcut to composing any DOS command.

Support for Multiple Menu Levels

1Dir+'s default operating mode includes two levels of menus. Additional command menus may be created to be accessed from existing menus or from other added menus.

When defining commands, you can specify which menu to return to when command execution is completed. In this way, you can return to the menu level from which the command was originally executed, or you can automatically return to the Main Menu.

Ready-Made Menus and Help Screens

As a menu and file management system, 1dir + is delivered with extensive file management menus already in place. By using the "point and shoot" method, the default menus may be all you need to run your applications and manage your files.

General and context-sensitive help screens are provided for each command in the file management menu system. These help screens may be edited and new ones may be added for new commands.

Password Security

Several levels of password security are available with 1dir+. Separate passwords may be assigned to separate commands and separate menus. Also, a master password may be assigned to protect access to the menu-builder and setup modules in addition to the security module used to assign and change passwords.

In the security module, you can totally disable or re-enable some of the more sophisticated options available with 1dir+, including the option to exit to DOS.

Speed of Execution

1dir + may be run as fully RAM-resident (to maximize speed) or partially resident (somewhat slower, but using one-fifth the amount of RAM). A third option releases all RAM when another application is executed and reloads the program when the application terminates.

Simple commands created through 1dir+ execute faster through 1dir + than a DOS batch file written entirely in ASCII. The makers of 1dir + also provide its command language and compiler (for a fee) to experts wanting additional power.

DOS COMMANDER

Connecticut Software Systems Corporation
30 Wilson Avenue
Rowayton, Connecticut 06853
Telephone: (203) 838-1844

Software Features

DOS Commander is a straightforward DOS menu utility that also includes several file management features. The following description focuses on the software's menu features. See Chapter 2 for a description of file management utilities in general.

Visual Display of Options

DOS Commander's display screen consists of three panels. On the left side of the screen is a list of function keys and short labels describing their purpose. These are ten of the 40 functions that may be assigned to these keys. Alternate functions can be viewed by pressing the Shift, Ctrl, or Alt keys.

The center panel contains an alphabetical file listing of the current directory. File names may be scrolled with the cursor keys. The currently selected file is highlighted. The right panel displays other information on directory, disk, and RAM use and the system date and time.

Minimal Keystroke Requirements

Commands assigned to function keys are executed with one or two keystrokes. The first ten options are run by pressing the function keys alone. The remaining 30 options are run by simultaneously pressing a Shift, Alt, or Ctrl key and a corresponding function key.

Executable files (those with COM, EXE, or BAT extensions) can be run by using the cursor keys to point to a selection and then pressing the <F1> (RUN) function key.

Subdirectories can be changed by using the cursor keys to point to the "target" subdirectory and then pressing the Return key.

Screen and Command Line Editing

DOS Commander provides 20 predefined function key settings and 20 user-defined function key settings, which are defined by assigning executable file names and labels to numbers from 1-20, corresponding to two function key sets.

DOS Commander provides no other text editing facility for creating batch files.

Assistance is provided for entering and editing DOS command lines. You can "bring down" any file name to the DOS command line by using the Insert key. The cursor keys can be used to edit a command line more extensively than with DOS alone.

Up to ten previously entered commands may be recalled, on a last-in, first-out basis, by pressing <Alt/1>.

Support for Multiple Menu Levels

DOS Commander provides no support for multiple-menu levels.

Ready-Made Menus and Help Screens

As mentioned previously, DOS Commander provides 20 predefined function key settings, which consist primarily of commonly used DOS internal and external commands. These settings are the basis of the file management features provided by DOS Commander.

In default mode, the predefined settings are assigned to the function keys <F1> through <F10> and <Shift/F1> through <Shift/F10>. The user-defined settings are assigned to <Alt/F1> through <Alt/F10> and <Ctrl/F1> through <Ctrl/F10>. The settings assigned to <F1> through <F10> are displayed on the screen unless you press Shift, Alt, or Ctrl from an empty command line.

DOS Commander provides an option to switch these function key assignments between predefined and user-defined. In this manner, ten user-defined function keys and labels will appear on the standard display screen.

On-line help is provided in two ways. A "ticker tape" line at the bottom of the screen provides context-sensitive help in entering command lines. In addition, the < Alt/Space Bar > key combination displays a pop-up window of help text, which overlaps the menu display screen.

The pop-up help screen text comes from an ASCII file and may be modified by any text editor that can produce straight ASCII files.

Password Security

Password security is provided for the system as a whole in the "Freeze Lock" feature. You select the password when you load the Freeze program. When leaving your computer, you press a preset pair of keys to "freeze" a predefined message display. When you return, enter the password to "unfreeze" the display.

While it is possible to deliberately defeat this security by rebooting the computer, this feature is useful for preventing accidental, unauthorized tampering.

Speed of Execution

DOS Commander remains RAM-resident during program execution. The manual further recommends copying the DOS COMMAND.COM file to a RAM disk to speed the execution of all DOS functions.

Other Features

DOS Commander also provides two other useful features. The Screen Saver empties the display screen (except for a moving time display) if no keyboard entry has been received for a preset number of seconds, which protects the monitor from phosphor burn-out. Pressing any key retrieves the display.

Another feature updates the system clock's time and date. The clock on an AT or compatible computer is actually reset with this utility. This feature eliminates the need to locate the setup diskette or, with some compatibles, to disconnect the battery to force the setup program.

THE NORTON COMMANDER

Peter Norton Computing, Inc.
2210 Wilshire Boulevard #186
Santa Monica, California 90403
Telephone: (213) 453-2361

Software Features

The Norton Commander is a file management utility and a DOS menu utility. The following description focuses on the software's menu features. See Chapter 2 for a more detailed description of The Norton Commander's file management features.

Visual Display of Options

The Norton Commander display screen consists of two side-by-side panels on the top half and the standard DOS prompt on the bottom half. Function key descriptions are listed across the bottom of the display.

Each panel may consist of a directory display or a display of disk, directory, and RAM status. Descriptive information about the directory may be entered and edited in the status panel. The directory display may contain only file names (three across) or more extensive file information (one across).

File names may be scrolled with the cursor keys. The currently selected file is highlighted.

Either panel, as well as the function key display, can be turned on or off.

When you select the user menu, i.e., press the <F2> key, the user menu pops up in a window overlapping the panel display.

Minimal Keystroke Requirements

Commands assigned to function keys are executed with one keystroke. Executable files (those with COM, EXE, or BAT extensions) can be run by the "point and shoot" method. Use the cursor keys to highlight your selection and press the Return key to execute it.

A user-defined menu screen will pop up when you press the <F2> function key. The menu options can be selected by pressing the corresponding character or "pointing and shooting."

If each panel represents a different subdirectory, the active subdirectory can be changed by switching panels.

A unique aspect of the Norton Commander is that the program is designed to be used with a mouse. The "point-and-shoot" feature lends itself to this type of input device. Using a mouse, of course, eliminates the need for any keyboard entry of information displayed on the screen.

Screen and Command Line Editing

The Norton Commander includes a relatively sophisticated text editor, which may be accessed by pressing the <F4> key. The text editor — or any other text editor that can produce ASCII files — can be used to create or edit the user menu.

Assistance is provided for entering and editing DOS command lines. You may "bring down" any file name to the DOS command line by pressing <Ctrl/Return>. The cursor keys and various Ctrl/key combinations can be used to edit a command line much more extensively than with DOS alone.

Previously entered commands may be recalled, on a last-in, first-out basis, by pressing ^E. Pressing ^X will scroll the list. Specific previous commands can be recalled by typing part of the command and pressing <Ctrl/Return>. The list of previous commands is searched for a match of the entered characters.

Support for Multiple Menu Levels

While The Norton Commander does not support a menu hierarchy, separate menus may be defined for separate directories. When you press the <F2> key to access the menu, the utility first searches the active directory. If no menu is found in the current directory, the default menu in the Norton Commander directory will be displayed.

Through the Setup screen, you may choose whether the user menu or standard Norton Commander screen should be displayed after a menu selection has been executed.

Ready-Made Menus and Help Screens

As mentioned previously, The Norton Commander provides ten predefined function key settings, which consist primarily of commonly used DOS internal and external commands. These settings are the basis of the file management features provided by The Norton Commander.

Help for using The Norton Commander is provided through the <F1> function key.

Password Security

The Norton Commander provides no password security feature.

Speed of Execution

The Norton Commander is not RAM-resident in the usual sense. Other applications can be run from within The Norton Commander. The program may be operated in one of two modes. The first mode maintains the entire program in RAM while other applications are run. Norton Commander operations perform faster in this mode.

The second mode releases all RAM when another application is executed and reloads the program when the application terminates. While reloading takes time, this mode eliminates potential RAM conflicts between programs and leaves more RAM available for the application.

EASY-DOS-IT

BMS Computer Inc.
375 North Wiget Lane, Suite 210
Walnut Creek, California 94598
Telephone: (415) 938-2620

Software Features

EASY-DOS-IT is a single-purpose but relatively powerful DOS menu utility program.

Visual Display of Options

The EASY-DOS-IT screen is a simple display of numbers on the left side and corresponding descriptions on the right side. At the bottom of the screen is a line of commands that may be accessed by a single highlighted letter. Each menu follows this format.

Minimal Keystroke Requirements

To select a menu option, press only the single digit corresponding to the menu line. Each menu contains up to nine selections. Subsequent menus are selected by entering "N" (for Next menu) from the command line at the bottom of the screen.

Replaceable parameters can be used in any command to limit the amount of necessary user input.

Screen and Command Line Editing

EASY-DOS-IT provides a public domain text editor that can be used to customize your menu system. The editor in EASY-DOS-IT is accessed by entering "M" (for Maintenance) from the command line at the bottom of the screen. Selections in the Maintenance menu access the parts of the system that you can edit.

Any text editor that can create ASCII files may be used. Three files may be edited: the menu file, the command file, and the submenu file.

In addition, EASY-DOS-IT provides a menu option to directly type in a DOS command.

Support for Multiple Menu Levels

EASY-DOS-IT supports multiple top-level menus and multiple second-level menus. Top-level menus are selected sequentially by entering "N" (for Next menu) or "B" for (Beginning menu). Submenus are selected by specific number from top-level menus.

These two features can be used to logically organize your menu system.

Ready-Made Menus and Help Screens

EASY-DOS-IT includes an extensive set of installed DOS menus, which include all commonly used DOS commands and several tutorial screens.

Tutorial or help screens can be created or edited through EASY-DOS-IT's text editor or any other editor that can produce ASCII files.

These screens are accessed much like other menu selections.

Password Security

EASY-DOS-IT offers two types of security. The first type adds a password to any menu selection. The password may be different for various menu selections.

The second type of security is provided through a configuration file that can disable access to DOS menus, Maintenance menus, or the DOS command line as well as disable the Exit-to-DOS command.

Speed of Execution

EASY-DOS-IT incorporates all changes in text file specifications when you run the Easymake maintenance option, which allows options to be performed faster than if they are continually searched for in text files.

DIRECT ACCESS

Delta Technology International, Inc.
1621 Westgate Rd.
Eau Claire, Wisconsin 54703
Telephone: (715) 832-7575

Software Features

Direct Access is a single-purpose menu utility that is easy to set up, easy to use, flexible, and fast.

Visual Display of Options

Direct Access provides a straightforward display screen that is gentle on the eyes. Menu options, each preceded by a letter, are listed vertically in a box in the center of the screen. Each menu may have up to 20 options. Function key descriptions below the list of options provide quick access to frequently used menu functions.

The time and date are displayed and updated at the bottom of each menu and submenu. The main menu has the additional feature of customizing the greeting (e.g., "Good Morning"), depending on the time of day.

Minimal Keystroke Requirements

Keystroke requirements are minimized in both setup and execution. As the menu configuration is set up, predefined templates are filled with standard, required information.

Executing menu selections often requires only one or, at most, two keystrokes. Commonly used DOS commands, complete with parameters, if possible, are provided in the DOS utilities menu.

Entering parameters is required only when maximum flexibility is desired.

Screen and Command Line Editing

Menu titles and selections can be easily edited through templates accessed through the Maintenance menu. Editing features are provided to insert, delete, and move menu selections.

The information required by the Main menu for each option is simply a description of the option and, if desired, a password. No special codes are required.

The information required by submenus consists of the program description, the location (if not the root directory of the default drive), and the command or commands to be executed. If the command consists of more than one line, a window pops up in which up to 20 command lines can be entered, much like creating a batch file.

Additional features are included for specifying prompts for diskette changes or command parameters.

Support for Multiple Menu Levels

Direct Access supports two menu levels. The first level contains the categories of application, and the second level for each category contains that category's specific applications.

Ready-Made Menus and Help Screens

Direct Access comes with a main menu that lists generic application categories. This menu can be used as is or modified as needed.

The DOS Utilities category also includes a submenu that includes several useful DOS commands, complete with descriptions and parameters. Like any other menu, this menu may be modified.

Password Security

Passwords can be used to restrict access to any submenu, application, menu maintenance, or exit-to-DOS command. Passwords are assigned separately for each of these functions, so they may vary by function, by application, and by submenu. You may try to enter the correct password three times before being denied access.

Speed of Execution

As mentioned previously, Direct Access is fast. Extra speed features allow you to bypass submenus if you type faster than your computer writes to the screen. In addition, if a submenu contains only one choice, the choice is automatically selected when the submenu is selected.

Other Features

Direct Access also includes a built-in logging system to track computer use by user and/or project. This feature may be turned on or off in the setup configuration.

Other Software in this Category

PROGRAM MANAGER

Lassen Software, Inc.
P.O. Box 1190
Chico, California 95927
Telephone: (916) 891-6957

DOSEASE

Software Solutions, Inc.
12 Cambridge Drive
Trumbull, Connecticut 06611
Telephone: (203) 374-8000

DOS-HELPER

Aristo Software
16811 El Camino Real #213
Houston, Texas 77058
Telephone: (800) 327-4786

TASK DIRECTOR

IBM Personally Developed Software
PO Box 3280
Wallingford, Connecticut 06494-3280
Telephone: (800) 426-7279

CHAPTER 5

MULTI-TASKING UTILITIES

Multi-tasking, which refers to simultaneously performing more than one computer task, is a term that has been overused and abused in the computer marketplace. The term has been applied to operations as simple as print-spooling and as complex as networking.

Within the context of this book, products are grouped not so much by how the programs accomplish results but by the comparability of the results. In this chapter, the focus is on utilities that make it possible to keep open more than one software application at the same time.

Even within this more narrow scope, two widely divergent multi-tasking approaches will be covered:

- windowing utilities (usually concurrent processors)
- task switchers (usually nonconcurrent processors)

Multi-tasking utility programs functionally overlap. Depending on the application software involved and the capabilities taken advantage of, the two types may offer minimal or great trade-offs.

THE PROBLEM

Three types of occasions call for multi-tasking capabilities:

- retrieving information from one application to use in another application

- interrupting one application to perform an unrelated task in another application

- working on one application while your computer independently processes another

Even if you work on only one project at a time, it may surprise you how many components comprise each project. In an entirely manual environment, you might have easy access to sales projection reports on your left and data in file cabinets on your right while you compose analytical comments on a pad of lined paper in front of you.

In a computerized environment, a single project might involve switching between spreadsheet analysis, data base examination, and word processing. The methods required to switch between applications may lead you to believe that your manual system was more productive.

Suppose, for example, you are entering accounting data and need information from a spreadsheet file to correctly allocate the entry. You may need to make a superfluous balancing entry to close your file, note where you left off, and exit the application through the menus. You must then switch directories and open the spreadsheet software, load the file, find your information, and write it down. Next, you must exit the spreadsheet software, move to and reload the accounting software, and begin where you left off. If you need the information again, all the steps must be repeated.

The same situation may occur if you must interrupt a long-term project to immediately finish an unrelated report.

As another example, suppose that you are "cleaning up" a large data base. You have marked several records for purging and are ready to condense and re-sort or index the large file. Depending on the application software, the contiguousness of files on your disk, and the size of your data base file, this operation could take anywhere from several minutes to over an hour. You can juggle your workload to time this operation to coincide with your lunch break or use the time to do non-computer work.

The same situation may occur if you are printing a long document, report, or several documents and reports in succession.

No truly simultaneous or concurrent processing exists with today's personal computer since each computer is typically equipped with only one processor; however, you may choose from several approaches to achieve some of the same effects, i.e., not having to rearrange your work habits to accommodate computer processing. Such approaches include the following:

- menus, batch files, and keyboard macros
- integrated software packages
- running one application from inside another
- RAM-resident desktop accessory overlays
- background utilities

Menu utilities, batch files, and/or macros may be used to minimize the number of keystrokes required to switch between application programs. After you complete processing in one application, one or two keystrokes can bring up the next application, configured for your specific use; however, none of these facilities will keep you from having to close files you are working with in one application before starting up another application.

Using internally integrated application software, like Framework and Symphony, can alleviate more of the problems inherent in switching between applications. Generally, two or more functions may be kept open at the same time, often visible in separate windows on your screen. Switching between the functional windows usually requires only one or two keystrokes.

Processing in one window must usually be completed before the software will respond to your command to switch windows. To achieve the benefits of internally integrated software, you are restricted to using the applications included in the package.

Some separate application software packages include facilities for running any other program, including another application, from within that application without closing its data files. Like integrated software, however, processing usually must be completed before the software will respond to commands to run another program.

Whether or not your applications will work well together in this manner depends on how each application addresses your hardware, RAM, and data files. Application software developers are not likely to have addressed the issue of compatibility in this particular situation, so you are urged to proceed with caution.

Desktop accessories in the form of RAM-resident utilities provide immediate access to several ancillary functions from within your application software. Easy access to a calculator, clock, calendar, notepad, and/or a cut and paste facility may often eliminate the need to close down one application, open another, and return to the first. Generally, application processing is suspended while accessories are in use.

Some time-consuming computer operations involve hardware rather than application software. While a data base Sort is performed almost exclusively by your data base management software, printing a data base report may be primarily a hardware operation. The time required to print a report depends more on the slower, mechanical operations of your printer than on your computer processing speed.

Similarly, many communications operations depend on the capacity of your modem and telephone lines and the efficiency of the receiving equipment. The instruction to send out information may be processed by your computer faster than the actual transmission can be performed.

These types of operations may be more efficiently performed in the "background." If the specific hardware operation can be separated from your application software, you can continue interacting with the application while printing or communication takes place.

Print spoolers, the DOS PRINT utility, and background communications programs all interact with your hardware independently of your application software. Generally, these facilities send information from a disk file or a RAM buffer that has received the application software output.

Using these methods, you can achieve limited switching ability and even concurrency without using multi-tasking utilities. With multi-tasking utilities, however, you can do more with greater flexibility.

MULTI-TASKING STRATEGY

Approach multi-tasking by first considering why you need the facility. You may discover new capabilities you never realized you could use; however, it is best not to experiment until you have achieved your original goals. Address the following issues in the context of your current requirements:

- choosing among utilities
- inter-utility cooperation
- RAM management
- data file management

Choosing Among Utilities

First, separate tasks requiring frequent user input from tasks that can be independently run for a long time. Note that some user input requirements may be entered in advance, depending on your application software's ability to read from the keyboard's type-ahead buffer.

For example, you may run three accounting reports (A, B, and C) consecutively from your menu at the close of each accounting period. Your application software may require for each report that you enter the selection key from the menu and press the Return key to indicate that the printer is set up. If your software is capable of reading from the keyboard buffer, you can enter

```
A
<return>
B
<return>
C
<return>
```

followed by the keys required to close the files and accounting application. You are then free to move on to another task while the computer prints your reports.

Note where functions of some utilities you are accustomed to using duplicate the capabilities of multi-tasking software. The more utilities you load into a computer, the more storage space and RAM are taken away from your application software. Furthermore, RAM-resident utilities that perform similar functions may confuse each other as well as the user.

If you are setting up a computer system from scratch, there is little reason to load two multi-tasking utilities. While you may want to use both a task switcher and a menu utility, you are unlikely to need a separate menu utility with a windowing utility. On the other hand, you may want both if you need several features that do not coexist on one utility, or if you are accustomed to one utility and another user of the same machine is accustomed to another.

You need windows if you must simultaneously view displays of two applications. You may only need a print spooler if you merely want to eliminate time wasted during printing.

Inter-Utility Cooperation

Once you have determined a configuration of utilities and application software, you must address how to use them together. Each program has its own requirements and behavior patterns, which may conflict with the requirements and behavior patterns of other programs.

Many utilities and software applications (as well as add-on and peripheral hardware) require certain statements in a CONFIG.SYS and/or AUTOEXEC.BAT file. Many applications require that certain files be present in your root directory or in a specific subdirectory, and many also specify a recommended loading order to minimize conflicts and achieve optimal performance.

Different CONFIG.SYS DEVICE statements can usually coexist in the same computer system. Generally, hardware device drivers should be loaded first. If one program cannot work with a device driver required by another program, the first program will usually provide a method to work around the conflict. In multi-tasking utilities, this situation occurs frequently with the ANSI.SYS device driver.

Other types of statements, however, are usually mutually exclusive. For example, only one FILES statement or one BUFFERS statement may exist in the system. If different software programs recommend different parameters for such statements, you should generally choose the higher parameter. Multi-tasking utilities, by nature, require a greater number of files to be simultaneously open than any single application.

Commands in the AUTOEXEC.BAT file depend on the directory location of the software, its command structure, and the desired loading order. The loading order is of particular importance to multi-tasking software.

Most RAM-resident software must be loaded before the application with which it will be used. Beyond this specification, manuals for RAM-resident utilities will recommend a preferred loading order in regard to other popular utilities.

Fulfilling each program's requirements can be confusing, especially when adding to your configuration new software not mentioned in other software manuals. For multi-tasking software in particular, some general concepts may be helpful.

If other RAM-resident utilities are loaded first, they cannot be controlled by multi-tasking software. In some multi-tasking software, other utilities may be accessible to every partition if they are loaded first, but they will not operate concurrently; all other processing stops when these utilities are called. In other multi-tasking software, if the other utilities are not loaded into a partition, they may not be accessible at all.

If another RAM-resident utility is loaded after multi-tasking software, it may be loaded into its own partition or into a partition coexisting with an application program. Desktop accessories, for example, may be accessible to all partitions from a separate partition. On the other hand, keyboard macro utilities can be operated with different macro files in several partitions containing application programs.

RAM Management

RAM management is a major aspect of multi-tasking utilities. Your operating system requires RAM. Utilities consume RAM. Your application software program files are loaded into RAM when called, and they fill as much RAM as possible with your data files because processing in RAM is much faster than reading from or writing to a disk.

With multi-tasking capabilities, several applications and their data files may be simultaneously open, filling up RAM several times faster than a single application. Depending on your RAM capacity and the software you use, this situation may slow some of your application processing and, without proper management, render other applications inoperable.

In most cases, you must enter the amount of RAM to be assigned to each partition. Manuals for your applications should list minimum and recommended RAM requirements. There are three components to the amount of required RAM:

- DOS overhead. Since multi-tasking utilities tend to incorporate a command processor (COMMAND.COM) in their overhead and use the same processor for each partition, you can discount this space requirement.

- Application program files and ancillary files, which must be loaded when you call them.

- Data files. Some applications can run with minimal space for data files by keeping more of the file on disk, if necessary. Spreadsheet software often requires the total worksheet file to be in RAM. Data base and word processing software tends to load portions of the file as needed and return other portions to the disk if there is insufficient RAM.

If you have limited RAM and/or "hungry" applications, your choice of multi-tasking software may be determined by the utilitiy's method of managing RAM. While some utilities "permanently" allocate RAM to each partition, others allow you to assign a portion of your disk space to "virtual memory."

Virtual memory is similar to (but really the opposite of) a virtual disk. Recall that a virtual disk or RAM disk is a portion of RAM set aside to store information and respond to read/write operations as if it were a disk. Virtual memory, on the other hand, is a portion of disk space set aside to store information in the format in which it was placed in RAM.

Virtual memory is used to switch inactive partitions to disk, freeing RAM for active partitions. If your computer has extended memory, you may achieve better results by creating a RAM disk to be used as virtual memory. Using a high-memory RAM disk results in no perceivable performance deterioration and frees up main memory for software that cannot access extended memory.

Data File Management

Multi-tasking requires that you exercise extra care with your data files. As always, open data files are vulnerable to hardware and software malfunctions. When operating in a multi-tasking environment, data files are particularly vulnerable for the following reasons:

- You may leave files open when you switch to another application.

- An application with open data files may not be visible on the screen.

- The higher number of software programs operating at one time increases the possibility of a conflict that will "freeze" your computer.

- It may be possible to open the same data file in more than one partition.

You already know you should close and save all data files by properly exiting the application before turning off the computer. You must perform the same steps for each application in each partition when leaving a multi-tasking environment.

Also be careful to close and save data files after viewing and/or processing them, even if you do not exit from the application. Take extreme care to exit correctly from each application before closing its partition.

One advantage of a multi-tasking environment is the ability to work with one application program in more than one partition, but this increases the danger of opening the same data file in more than one partition.

If you make changes to a data file in one partition and open the same file in another partition before closing the file in the first partition, you will see the unmodified file in the second partition. If you save the file from both partitions, the last version saved will usually overwrite the first.

If you approach multi-tasking with caution, you can avoid the dangers and discover ways to work around problems. The utilities described in the following sections provide a number of tools that allow your computer to work more efficiently with multi-tasking operations.

THE UTILITIES

The multi-tasking utilities described in this chapter fall into one of two categories:

- windowing utilities
- task-switchers

The two categories include overlapping features. The following chart summarizes the general differences between the features in each type of utility.

	Windows	Switchers
Partitioning		
concurrent processing	mostly yes	mostly no
view more than one partition at a time	mostly yes	mostly no
control window size	mostly yes	mostly full-screen
cut and paste between partitions	mostly yes	mostly no
Compatibility and installation		
compatibility issues	many problems	fewer problems
installation ease	may be difficult	may be easier
Memory management		
overhead memory required	100-200K	under 50K
use extended memory	mostly yes though mostly as RAM disk	mostly yes though mostly as RAM disk
use virtual memory	mostly yes	mostly no
User interface		
user-definable menu system	mostly yes	mostly no
support mouse	mostly yes	mostly no
other features	mostly yes	mostly no

Partitioning

All multi-tasking software works by partitioning RAM. The number of partitions allowed by the various multi-tasking utilities ranges from two to ten to the limits of your hardware. Applications and their data files may be loaded into the separate partitions without fear of their being overwritten by each other.

The user controls the amount of RAM allocated to each partition. Some utilities allow you to alter the amount of allocated RAM for one or more partitions without unloading all of the partitions first.

Only one partition can be in the "foreground" at one time. The foreground is the area with which the user is interacting via the keyboard or other entry device. The remaining partitions are considered to be in the background. The user can switch between partitions with one keystroke or keystroke combination or one click of a mouse.

Windowing utilities, as is evident by their name, can display more than one partition at a time, each in an individual window on your display screen. Generally, the user is given a great deal of control over the size and position of the windows on the screen. Switching from one window to another, with one keystroke, is equivalent to switching partitions.

Some of the task-switching utilities, which do not provide windows per se, can make use of two separate monitors to display two different partitions.

Several multi-tasking utilities, primarily those with windows, allow "cutting and pasting" between partitions, which means that a portion of the display—text or graphic—can be marked in one partition and copied to a specific location in another partition.

Some multi-tasking software provides for concurrent processing with compatible applications and DOS operations. In this context, concurrency is defined as the ability to leave a partition in mid-process—sorting, printing, searching, calculating, disk-formatting, etc.—without halting the processing in order to enter or view other information and start other computer processes.

Most of the time, the operations you will be performing in different partitions will not compete with each other for the same processing area at the same time. The multi-tasking software regulates the competition when it does arise, allowing the operations to take turns with the processor.

When processes are in competition, each individual application may process somewhat more slowly than it would otherwise. This slowdown has much less of an impact than the time it would take for the user to regulate the situation. Some multi-tasking utilities do allow the user to set priorities among the partitions so that one partition may receive more time per turn than others.

Some multi-tasking utilities allow you to load and begin processing directly on software in a background partition without requiring you to switch out of the foreground partition.

Compatibility and Installation

To perform their magic, multi-tasking utilities take advantage of every capability offered by your computer's operating system. For this reason, they require that your operating system perform according to expectations and that your hardware and software work through your operating system. When these expectations are not met, which frequently occurs, you cannot take full advantage of the utilities.

Window utilities control much more of your computer's RAM, processors, display, and keyboard than task switchers; therefore, they present more compatibility problems than task switchers with nonstandard hardware and with application software that also wants to be in control.

Before you purchase a multi-tasking utility, you should check that your hardware and your favorite or important software are compatible with the utility.

Regarding hardware, note that some window utilities require that your monitor adaptor board have graphics capabilities. Some have stringent IBM compatibility requirements. A few utilities will not work well or require special settings with turbo boards.

Multi-tasking utilities generally can be run on either a hard disk or floppy diskette system. For the most part, hard disks are recommended to store all those applications that can be accessible simultaneously. A few of these utilities provide a feature that will alert you when a diskette for an active partition has been removed.

Software compatibility issues are more numerous; however, the multi-tasking utilities offer work-around solutions wherever possible. In other cases, the utilities may still function but with limitations on some of their features.

Window utilities work much more reliably and advantageously with application software written to their specifications; however, since no standard has emerged, many application software developers have not accepted the burden of redesigning their software to meet the window utilities' requirements.

Applications that bypass DOS to write directly to the screen or take over the keyboard present the most frequent problems. Such applications, though described as "misbehavers," have their reasons for taking direct control. The operating system may limit their speed and flexibility, and their performance may deteriorate if they follow the rules.

The concurrency feature also causes frequent compatibility problems with direct screen writers. Screen output sent while the software is processing in the background cannot be intercepted and redirected by the multi-tasking software; therefore, the screen output tends to "come through" to the foreground partition and any other windows currently on the screen.

Multi-tasking utilities often supply work-around solutions for the most popular culprits. These include DEBUG programs that actually modify the application software and special loading modules to be used when bringing up the specific application.

Other solutions involve special configuration settings, usually for the utility rather than for the application software, giving a direct screen-writing application the full screen whenever that application is active or, conversely, suspending the application's processing whenever it is not in the foreground, or its window is smaller than the full screen.

The multi-tasking software itself may be so "well-behaved" that one multi-tasking utility may be loaded in one of the partitions of another multi-tasking utility. The result, though manageable by the utility software, may be more confusing than helpful for the user.

There is usually no problem running a multi-tasking utility from its own subdirectory. The major requirement is that the utility usually needs access to the COMMAND.COM file. This access may be automatic if COMMAND.COM is in the root directory of the default drive or is reachable via a path statement. Otherwise, you may use the DOS environment command SET COMSPEC= to inform the utility of COMMAND.COM's location.

Memory Management

The multi-tasking utilities offer different facilities for managing RAM, some that are transparent to the user and others that the user may control.

The windowing utilities tend to consume more overhead memory than the task-switching utilities. This consumption may be lessened somewhat if you choose not to take advantage of all of the utility's bells and whistles.

The amount of RAM used by the applications during your operations depends mainly on the application but also on the way the multi-tasking utility works. If the utility makes use of the virtual memory concept described earlier, more RAM is available for the active software. In this case, you may actually assign more total RAM to your partitions than you physically have in your computer.

Some use of virtual memory may be controlled by the user. Usually, you can specify both the amount of real RAM to be assigned to the partition as well as the amount of disk space that can be used for virtual RAM. Those multi-tasking utilities that can address extended memory will also allow you to specify whether to use real disk space or RAM disk space for virtual memory.

Most multi-tasking utilities allow you to choose which partitions may be swapped with virtual memory. Some nonconcurrent processors can automatically unload every partition to virtual memory, slowing down the switching a bit, but leaving all of your RAM available to the active partition. Note, however, that communications software should never be swapped with virtual memory.

When assigning the amount of RAM to be allocated to a given partition, there are some considerations that may be specific to the particular multi-tasking software you are using. The amount of RAM available will vary inversely with the amount of overhead RAM consumed by the utility. The amount of RAM the utility requires to operate each partition may be added automatically or may need to be incorporated into your specifications.

Depending on the utility's use of the DOS command processor, you may or may not have to apportion space for it in any partition. Usually you must assign extra memory for a graphics screen save (to duplicate information stored on a graphics card), but the amount may vary from one utility to another. If the utility can access ROM BASIC, BASIC applications will require less RAM than they would otherwise.

Several multi-tasking utilities take advantage of extended RAM in one or more of the following ways:

- as a RAM disk for virtual memory

- when accessible by application software that can access extended memory without multi-tasking

- when accessed by multi-tasking software itself

User Interface

Windowing utilities tend to be menu-driven while task switchers tend to be command-driven. Some utilities in each category offer a choice of menu or command interface.

Window software replaces the interface of your entire operating system. The DOS interface may be menu-oriented, use icons, or be command-driven. The menu systems may be as customized as those described in Chapter 4, "DOS Menu Utilities." Most menu utilities support a mouse input device.

All of these multi-tasking utilities can be automatically loaded from your AUTOEXEC.BAT file. In addition, they usually may be preconfigured to automatically load your applications into specific partitions.

Several of these multi-tasking utilities include ancillary features as optional add-on packages or actual features of the utility software itself. The add-ons can preclude the need to crowd your computer with additional, less compatible utilities.

Other features frequently include desktop accessories such as an alarm clock, calendar, calculator, notepad, card file, and autodialer. In addition, important add-ons such as communications software and keyboard macro utilities are also provided.

The specific features of each utility program are described in the following sections.

MICROSOFT WINDOWS

Microsoft Corporation
16011 NE 36th Way, Box 97017
Redmond, Washington 98073-9717
Telephone: (206) 882-8088

Software Features

Partitions

Microsoft Windows has no predefined limit to the number of partitions that can be opened at one time. As many applications as can fit in your computer's memory (or virtual memory) can be simultaneously loaded.

Program information files (PIF files) can be created or edited to configure each partition for a particular application. Several predefined PIF files are included for popular software applications.

The partitions are displayed in "tiled" (as opposed to overlapping) windows on the screen. The window size may be adjusted at any time to control how much of the display can be seen. A window can be removed from the display (and indicated as an icon at the bottom of the screen) without actually closing the window.

In Microsoft Windows, you can transfer information between partitions. Information is stored on its Clipboard feature between selecting and copying functions so that information can be transferred between applications that are not simultaneously displayed. Information may be transferred from any application and to any application that can run in a window.

Microsoft Windows supports concurrent background processing for any application that can run in windows, i.e., not direct screen-writers or those requiring full memory. Applications that can run in windows may be loaded directly into the background.

Compatibility and Installation

Microsoft Windows requires a graphics adaptor card. An IBM Enhanced Graphics Adaptor or compatible card is required to run the utility in color.

Any software application that can run in DOS can run with Microsoft Windows; however, most Windows features are not available to applications that directly address the screen or keyboard or that require full memory. These programs will generally only run nonconcurrently in full-screen mode, rather than in windows; processing will be suspended on other applications as these applications are run and suspended on these applications when others are run.

Other RAM-resident utilities work best with Windows if loaded before Windows; however, Windows does provide a special setting to allow such utilities to be run with an application from within Windows, although conflicts may occur.

Memory Management

A PIF file setting can be used to allocate a specific amount of RAM or all available RAM to an application.

If Windows finds insufficient RAM to run an application, it will switch other open applications to virtual memory on disk. The amount of space set aside for virtual memory will default to the space required by the first switch, unless otherwise specified. The switching feature may be entirely disabled.

Extended memory can be used to set up a RAM disk for virtual memory. If no drive letter is specified, virtual memory will be set up on the default hard disk. A floppy diskette *cannot* be used as virtual memory.

A built-in print spooler moderates printing activity in the background.

User Interface

Microsoft Windows provides an alternative DOS interface that can be run by keyboard or mouse. Selections are made from pop-down menus or from icons displayed on a bar across the bottom of the screen.

The entire screen is always in use either by full-screen applications or by a combination of applications in windows and a DOS file management window displaying the current directory or selected files.

Microsoft Windows provides built-in desktop accessory features including a calculator, calendar, clock, card file, notepad, and communications software.

TASKVIEW

Sunny Hill Software
P.O. Box 33711
Seattle, Washington 98133-3711
Telephone: (206) 367-0650

Software Features

Taskview is a task-switcher that provides concurrent processing for and data transfer between up to ten applications.

Partitions

Taskview supports ten active partitions. One partition is in the foreground, i.e, the user can interact with it at any given time. The remaining partitions continue processing in the background.

Program forms filled in by the user configure each partition for the particular application to be run. Several sample program forms are included in the manual for popular software applications.

Taskview provides a separate program that can be used to transfer information between partitions. Information is stored between selecting and copying functions so that information may be transferred between applications not simultaneously active.

Taskview supports concurrent background processing for most applications and DOS operations. By default, the foreground operation has processing priority so that user interaction is not slowed. Separate priorities can be set for each partition's background processing.

Compatibility and Installation

Taskview does not require a graphics adaptor card.

Taskview provides special loader files for some popular application software programs that write directly to the screen. These loader files will allow these applications to run concurrently in the background. Background processing is suspended for other direct screen writers and for applications that take control of the keyboard.

Other RAM-resident utilities may be loaded before or after Taskview. Taskview documentation recommends different loading orders for different types of utilities. Generally, if loaded before Taskview, they can be accessed from any partition but may halt all background processing when directly accessed. If loaded after Taskview, they may be loaded in separate partitions or in partitions with other applications.

Other multi-tasking utilities, including window utilities, can be loaded in Taskview partitions, although they may not be permitted to run in the background.

Memory Management

The program information form is used to specify the minimum and optimal amounts of RAM required to run an application. Taskview attempts to allocate the optimal amount but will run the application as long as the minimum RAM is available.

If Taskview finds insufficient RAM to run an application, it will switch other open applications to virtual memory on disk. This switching feature may be disabled for individual partitions.

Extended memory can be used to set up a RAM disk that will be used for virtual memory. If no drive letter is specified, virtual memory will be set up on the default hard disk.

Extended memory can also be used by the Taskview menu system.

User Interface

Taskview can be run in menu or in command mode. In menu mode, the program information form is displayed on the screen for you to fill in when a partition is opened. A program file can be made permanent by adding it to the user-defined program menu.

In command mode, program information may be entered as parameters on the command line. These commands may be run from batch files.

A mouse input device is supported.

Taskview includes two ancillary programs. SMACS.COM is a keyboard macro utility, and CP.COM is a cut-and-paste utility.

Taskview adds enhanced editing capabilities to the DOS command line.

DESQVIEW

Quarterdeck Office Systems
150 Pico Boulevard
Santa Monica, California 90405
Telephone: (213) 392-9851

DESQview is primarily a window utility.

Partitions

The number of open partitions supported by DESQview is limited by hardware capacity long before it is limited by the utility itself.

Program information files (DVP files) may be created or edited to configure each partition for the particular application to be run. Several predefined DVP files are included for popular software applications.

The partitions are displayed as windows on the screen. The window size may be adjusted at any time to control how much of the display can be seen. A window may be hidden or "put aside" to virtual memory without actually closing the window.

The <Ctrl/Alt/Del> key combination aborts the current partition and closes the window. <Ctrl/Shift/Del> reboots the entire system to reconfigure partitions.

DESQview contains a sophisticated transfer facility that allows you to transfer disjointed blocks of information in text or numerical form between any partitions, edit the information, and store the procedure to be repeated at a later time.

DESQview supports concurrent background processing for any applications that can run in windows, i.e., not direct screen-writers or those requiring full memory. Applications that can run in windows may be loaded directly into the background. The facility for background processing may be turned off for any individual partition.

Compatibility and Installation

DESQview does not require a graphics adaptor card but is fully functional with most color/graphics cards.

DESQview supplies application program patches and/or loaders for several popular direct screen-writing programs. Other direct screen-writing application programs may be run in full-screen-only mode. These programs may be viewed with suspended processing in smaller windows.

DESQview automatically provides the ANSI.SYS file for each partition that can be used independently for each program that does not write directly to screen.

Other RAM-resident utilities may be loaded before or after DESQview. DESQview documentation recommends different loading orders for different types of utilities. Generally, if loaded before DESQview, they can be accessed from any partition but may halt all background processing when directly accessed. If loaded after DESQview, they may be loaded in their own separate partitions or in partitions with other applications, and swapped to disk when not in use.

IBM TopView PIF files (program information files) may be used interchangeably with DESQview DVP files.

Memory Management

A DVP file setting may be used to allocate a specific amount of RAM or all available RAM to an application.

If DESQview finds insufficient RAM to run an application, it will switch other open applications to virtual memory on disk. This switching feature may be entirely disabled or disabled for individual partitions.

Extended memory may be used as a print spooler and/or as a RAM disk to be used for virtual memory. If no drive letter is specified, virtual memory will be set up on the default hard disk.

DESQview can use certain extended memory boards for concurrent background processing. Any applications that can otherwise make use of extended memory can use extended memory through DESQview.

User Interface

DESQview provides an alternative DOS interface that can be run by keyboard or mouse. Selections are made from pop-down menus. You may add or edit information regarding programs to the Program Location menu.

The utility includes DOS file management features, its own keyboard macro utility, and an auto-dialer. Optional DESQview features include a calculator, calendar, and notepad as well as communications software.

MEMORY/SHIFT

North American Business Systems, Inc.
3840 Lindell Boulevard
St. Louis, Missouri 63108
Telephone: (314) 534-7404

Software Features

Memory/Shift is an uncomplicated, easy-to-use task-switcher.

Partitions

Memory/Shift supports up to nine partitions. Each partition may be given a name of up to sixteen characters.

You may switch between partitions by selecting the specific partition to make active or by toggling through all open partitions.

The <Ctrl/Alt/Del> key combination aborts the current partition and closes the window. <Ctrl/Shift/Del> reboots the entire system to reconfigure partitions.

Only one partition is visible at a time, unless you use two monitors. In this case, the first partition is automatically assigned to the first monitor, and other partitions may be viewed one at a time on the second monitor.

In Memory/Shift, you can transfer up to 3,000 characters between any partitions with the program's data transfer facility. Information from more than one partition can be added to the transfer buffer before it is placed. The same information may be placed in any partition a number of times.

Memory/Shift does not provide concurrent processing. Processing is suspended in one partition when another partition is made active.

Compatibility and Installation

Memory/Shift does not require a graphics adaptor card to run.

When using Memory/Shift with floppy diskettes, the utility provides a disk-checking feature to verify that the proper diskettes are in the proper drives.

Since there is no concurrent processing, there are virtually no compatibility problems.

Other RAM-resident utilities work best if loaded before Memory/Shift.

Memory Management

Fixed amounts of RAM are user-allocated as the partitions are created. Memory/Shift offers some RAM conservation by using the same DOS command processor for all partitions. An additional 6K of RAM must be allocated for each partition after the second one.

Memory/Shift does not use virtual memory.

User Interface

Memory/Shift may be configured with an interactive installation routine or directly from a DOS command line, which may be called from the AUTOEXEC.BAT file.

Memory/Shift's individual partitions may be automatically loaded with the desired applications via standard batch files — named AUTOEXE1.BAT, AUTOEXE2.BAT, and so on — that correspond to the partitions.

On-line help is available with a keystroke.

Desk/Shift, a companion utility, offers compatible desktop accessories such as a calculator, alarm clock, calendar, notepad, and clipboard as well as communications software.

DOUBLEDOS

SoftLogic Solutions, Inc.
One Perimeter Road
Manchester, New Hampshire 13103
Telephone: (800) 272-9900

DoubleDOS is a task-switcher that provides concurrent processing for two applications.

Partitions

DoubleDOS supports two active partitions that can be toggled back and forth and simultaneous printing operations for up to four printers.

Only one partition is visible at a time unless you use two monitors, in which case one partition is displayed on each monitor.

Each partition may be directed to a different printer. If the DOS PRINT background printer is loaded after DoubleDOS in each partition, each partition can use separate background printing as well.

DoubleDOS provides for concurrent processing with most applications. You may specify processing priority for either partition in a two-to-one ratio or specify equal time for each. At any time, the background processing can be suspended or resumed.

Compatibility and Installation

DoubleDOS does not require a graphics adaptor card to run.

DoubleDOS supplies application program patches and drivers for many popular direct screen-writing applications. For other potential conflicts, the utility supplies an alternative to suspending background processing. This feature constantly and imperceptibly refreshes the active partition's display, quickly cleaning up any background screen-writing a fraction of a second after it occurs.

DoubleDOS also provides for manually switching display modes through the menu to reset application programs that switch modes without informing the operating system.

DoubleDOS provides a version of ANSI.SYS that allows for each partition to independently use that file's keyboard remapping function. The DoubleDOS version can be permanently substituted since it works identically to ANSI.SYS when DoubleDOS is not being run.

Other RAM-resident utilities must be loaded within a DoubleDOS partition to be used with the application software in the partition.

Memory Management

Fixed amounts of RAM are user-allocated as the partitions are created. You specify the size of one partition, and DoubleDOS automatically assigns the remaining available RAM to the other partition.

You can change the memory allocation (without reinstalling the utility) when no applications are running.

DoubleDOS does not use virtual memory.

DoubleDOS supplies its own printer buffer, which may be set for 1K to 64K.

User Interface

DoubleDOS may be run in menu or command mode. In menu mode, you can specify either long (including a status display) or short (freeing up more allocable RAM). In command mode, DoubleDOS can be loaded from the AUTOEXEC.BAT file.

DoubleDOS commands can be written in a file named DDCON-FIG.SYS to automatically set up the original configuration.

Other features included in DoubleDOS include a screen-saver with a dimming interval that can be specified in numbers of minutes and an extended keyboard buffer of 128 characters.

Other Software in this Category

TOPVIEW

International Business Machines Corporation
1133 Westchester Avenue
White Plains, New York 10604
Telephone: (914) 765-1900

CONCURRENT PC DOS

Digital Research, Inc.
60 Garden Court
Monterey, California 93942
Telephone: (408) 649-3896

SOFTWARE CAROUSEL

SoftLogic Solutions, Inc.
530 Chestnut Street
Manchester, New Hampshire 01301
Telephone: (800) 272-9900

E-Z-DOS-IT

Hammer Computer Systems, Inc.
900 Larkspur Landing Circle, Suite 250
Larkspur, California 94939
Telephone: (415) 461-7633

CHAPTER 6

KEYBOARD MACRO UTILITIES

The primary function of keyboard macro utilities is to redefine the computer's interpretation of keystrokes or keystroke combinations. By stretching the implementation of this basic function, the utilities frequently include predefined macros that provide features usually found in other types of utilities.

For the most part, this chapter will concentrate on the most basic macro function. But other related features will be discussed in context.

There are three basic conceptual elements in personal computing:

- input
- processing
- output

This chapter focuses on the first element —**input**. There are several types of input devices that may be used to enter information into your computer, such as keyboards, mice, touch-sensitive screens, drawing pads, and optical readers. Keyboard entry is, of course, the most commonly used method.

Each keyboard contains its own **microprocessor**, which translates keystrokes into machine code. The keystroke interpretation, as opposed to the keyboard layout, is the determining factor of machine or software compatibility. Keystroke interpretation occurs at three distinct points in the normal course of computing:

- At the keyboard level, each key sends up to four distinct **scan** codes to the computer when the user presses the key by itself or in conjunction with pressing the Shift, Ctrl, or Alt keys.

- At the operating system level, each scan code is translated into a specific ASCII code.

- At the software level, each ASCII code determines a specific software response.

The software response to a keystroke combination is the level at which the keyboard directly affects the computer user. As long as the keyboard's scan codes are consistent, the keyboard layout has virtually no impact on software response.

THE PROBLEM

There are a number of keyboard interpretation issues with which computer users find fault. Issues are found at each point of the interpretation process:

- layout inconsistency and inefficiency
- number of keystrokes required
- command inconsistency

Layout Inconsistency and Inefficiency

Standard keyboard layouts vary among brands of computers and among models within the same brand. In addition, keyboards with nonstandard layouts may be purchased separately from computers to satisfy a variety of specific requirements.

Before microcomputers, the keyboard console was generally viewed as one of the two major components (along with the display screen) of a relatively low-cost computer terminal rather than as an integral part of the computer itself. Software was designed with specific keyboard console models in mind, and variations in keyboards were designed with specific software in mind.

An obvious example is a keyboard belonging to a dedicated word processor. This single application computer provides fewer key code possibilities and less flexibility. The layout of the keyboard is determined by the ease of access required for keys frequently used by the typist.

Personal microcomputers, with their general-purpose focus, are designed to be used with a large number of different software programs designed for various applications; therefore, a keyboard designed for maximum efficiency with one software program may not be ideal for another. As a result, a more general-purpose layout is designed.

A user switching from a dedicated word processor to a personal computer may find the new keyboard layout as disorienting as the new software. Similarly, as the design of this general-purpose layout is improved, users switching between models may also find the transition difficult. This inconsistency is even more confusing when two or more computers and/or typewriters co-exist in the same office.

The variations in keyboard layout are primarily the result of different ideas of layout efficiency. Layout efficiency is defined by software requirements as well as by general ergonomics — or the comfort factor.

There are three basic ergonomic issues:

- relative size of keys
- relative position of keys
- number of keys

Variations in the relative size of the keys can prevent mistakes during input. For example, computer users often prefer that the Return key be larger than the other keys to provide faster, error-free access.

The relative position of the keys can have the same impact. There tends to be less space between the keys on computer keyboards than on typewriters, causing more errors for computer users accustomed to typewriters.

The numeric key pad on the right side of the keyboard may cause problems for left-handed users. The function keys on the left of the keyboard may feel unfamiliar if you are used to function keys positioned across the top of the keyboard.

Similarly, many computer users, especially those without full use of ten fingers, find typing easier on a DVORAK rather than the standard QWERTY (named for the first six letters on the top alpha row of the keyboard) layout. The DVORAK layout was developed by studying the relative frequency of use of each letter of the alphabet in the English language. The more frequently used letters were then positioned for easier access. The DVORAK layout is also available in left-handed or right-handed versions.

Access to certain key codes requires that you simultaneously press more than one key. For example, to enter an uppercase letter, you must press and hold down the Shift key while also pressing an alpha key. The evolution of Shift key use on typewriters has produced a CapsLock key and a Shift key on either side of the alpha keys.

This evolution has not been applied to the Ctrl or Alt keys, which may be difficult to reach simultaneously with another key. Note also that the reboot routine requires that you simultaneously press three keys— <Ctrl>, <Alt>, and <Del>. For the many computer users who have manual impairments, these key combinations can be impossible.

The quantity of keys also makes a difference in computing ease. The quantity of keys is kept low to conserve space and make every key easily accessible; however, this ease of access is partly defeated by some keys having to perform more than one common function. In this case, an extra keystroke is required to switch functions, for example, pressing the Shift key to enter a number from the cursor/numeric keypad.

Command Inconsistency

Software developers enjoy total flexibility with regard to keystroke interpretation. This flexibility, however, is the root of many problems. While much software follows certain logical or historical conventions, small variations between applications may contribute to many input errors.

For example, compare the results of the following keystrokes and combinations in dBASE III and Wordstar 3.3:

Keys	dBASE III PLUS	Wordstar 3.3
<Del>	delete character above cursor	delete character to the left of cursor
<Backspace>	delete character to the left of cursor	move one character to the left of cursor
^Y	delete characters to right of cursor	delete entire line

It is easy to see how you could accidentally lose valuable information by using the keystrokes required by one application to perform the same function in another.

Number of Keystrokes Required

If your software application is written efficiently, most universally common commands can be executed with one or two keystrokes; however, you may routinely perform sequences of commands peculiar to your needs.

For example, your standard document format may include routinely indenting certain paragraphs by two tab spaces and printing them in boldface type. Depending on your word processing software, this procedure could easily require up to fifteen keystrokes each time it is used.

Print enhancements, such as boldface and underlining, require special care. In most word processing programs, you must mark both the beginning and the end of the enhanced text. If you forget one of the markers, the resulting document may be entirely underlined or otherwise enhanced. While this result is sometimes comical, it can also be a nuisance.

Similarly, timed communications operations also may require keyboard entry both before and after the communication itself. If the computer user is not available at the required time, the operation may be left hanging in the middle until much later.

In another example, the repetitive keystrokes may be a string of text rather than a sequence of commands. When you are constantly adding to a data base names, addresses, and telephone numbers from a single geographical area, you may spend a great deal of time entering the same city, state, zip code, and area code.

Many software applications provide their own facilities for defining keys to perform exactly these types of functions. The function keys or some other key combinations may be defined by the user as follows:

Software	Definition methods
DOS	ANSI.SYS command sequences to redefine any key
dBASE III Plus	dBASE commands to define function keys
WordStar	configuration program to define function keys and certain other key combinations
Lotus	macro commands to define Alt keys

Not all software applications offer these features. Those that do usually limit user-definable keys to function keys and a few specific key combinations. The number of characters that may be entered to create the new definition is often severely limited. In addition, the methods of key redefinition are completely different in different applications.

MACRO STRATEGY

Macros add another layer of interpretation between the operating system and the software. In this layer, the ASCII code may be changed to a completely different ASCII code. In this manner, you may control the definition of each key.

You can disable keys, swap key definitions, add foreign or graphics characters to your keyboard, define one key to display pages of help text, build a menu system, or define one key to run an entire program. The possibilities can be overwhelming. The opportunity for easing your computing life is enormous, but so is the potential for making life more complicated.

As with many other categories of utilities (see Chapters 4 and 5 on path and menu utilities), you should start slowly. Begin with what you already know you want. The most clever shortcut is no time-saver if you cannot remember how to execute it. Similarly, if one solution causes new problems, you have made no progress.

There are five basic areas where keyboard macros provide assistance:

- standardizing the keyboard layout
- standardizing application software commands
- minimizing keystrokes
- expanding keystrokes
- minimizing typing errors

Standardizing the Keyboard Layout

There are several reasons why you might want to rearrange the layout of your computer's keyboard. Most of these reasons involve keeping the layout familiar rather than striving for the ergonomic ideal. You may want to alter your computer keyboard layout to minimize differences if one or more of the following situations occur:

- You are switching back and forth between your computer and a typewriter.

- Your office has more than one computer with different keyboards.

- You are developing, testing, or documenting programs that will be used with different keyboards.

● You switch to a new computer with a different keyboard layout.

● You find a DVORAK layout preferable to the QWERTY layout.

Standardizing Application Software Commands

There are few standards adhered to in applications software commands. Different applications frequently require unique command sequences to perform identical functions. As you have previously seen, the more similar these commands are, the more dangerous their differences are.

Macros may be used with your software applications to achieve identical results from identical command sequences. For example, one function key or one Alt key combination may be programmed to quit each application and return to the root directory. Similarly, the Del and Backspace keys and other editing key combinations may be programmed to operate identically in all applications.

There are two advantages to using keyboard macro utility programs over an application's own customizing facilities:

● Macro utilities have fewer limitations and more flexibility than application-customizing facilities.

● In addition to standardizing the application commands, the use of macro utilities standardizes the method of defining macros.

Minimizing Keystrokes

One of the major joys of macros is that they eliminate repetitive typing. Macros may contain a great deal more information than is required simply to swap the definition of one key with another. Entire programs or pages of text may be included in a single macro. This facility is useful both within and outside of applications software. Useful macro implementations include the following:

- condensing frequently used, long application keystroke sequences into one command

- building menu systems for easier access to all of your applications

Condensing keystroke sequences within an application is equally useful for text and command input. With spreadsheet software, for example, you may write one macro to set printer control codes or format and fill in a date field. With one keystroke, you may then add this macro to any worksheet.

When using data base software, suppose you are constantly adding prospect information to a data base of potential clients in the New York City area. To save time repeating keystrokes required for Manhattan residents, you may program one key to do the following:

- enter the total character string, "New York, New York"
- automatically move to the next field
- enter the first two characters of New York City zip codes
- prompt yourself for the rest of the zip code
- move to the next field
- enter the area code

With word processing software, you may define a macro as an entire boilerplate letter, which will prompt you for variable information. You may also find useful a macro that consists of beginning and ending print formatting commands with a variable in between.

Macros may be used outside of your applications software to build a menu system for easier access to all of your applications as well as to frequently used DOS commands. If you are using macros for other purposes, you can easily extend your implementation for these purposes.

You may, for example, assign application access routines to function keys for one keystroke operation. With nested macros, you can design multiple menu levels. (See Chapter 5, "DOS Menu Utilities," for programs designed specifically for this purpose.)

Expanding Keystrokes

There are some situations where, rather than minimizing keystrokes, you will want to increase them. Two very different situations that call for expanding keystrokes are as follows:

- confirmation of input before execution
- one-finger typing

Many times during the operation of a software application, user input is required. Sometimes, just a one-character entry is requested, and other times, a user is requested to fill in a blank field. Sometimes, software will require confirmation after the input—for example, pressing the Return key—before the program will resume.

Other times, however, as long as any key is pressed or the input field is filled up, the program resumes without confirmation. If you find this situation is causing too many erroneous inputs, you may want to define a macro that requires confirmation by having the user press a specific key. When confirmation is required, you are given a second chance to examine and edit your input before the program resumes.

One-finger typing refers to the altering of commands using simultaneous key combinations so that they may be entered sequentially. <Ctrl><PrtSc>, for example, would be entered by pressing the <Ctrl> key, releasing it, and then pressing the <PrtSc> key. Manually impaired computer users may find this typing mode helpful while others may prefer to stay with simultaneous keystrokes most of the time.

Minimizing Typing Errors

Many typing errors are caused primarily by the keyboard layout. When the keys are so close together, it is not uncommon to reach for one key and, by mistake, press another one in close proximity. Many such typographical errors may be easily corrected with no harm done, but others may have inconvenient consequences. Three common errors of this type include the following:

- Pressing the <Esc> key when, on a PC keyboard, you are reaching for <F2>, the number 1, or the <Tab> key. An untimely Escape command may interrupt a program or a printout.

- Pressing the open apostrophe (`) key when you mean to press the closed apostrophe (') key or the <Return> key. This mistake is innocuous most times, but some software and printers will misinterpret this key and produce undesired results.

- Pressing the <Shift> and <PrtSc> keys simultaneously when you are reaching for the asterisk (*). This mistake can easily occur even on a keyboard where the two keys have been separated; you may, for example, hold down the <Shift> key to use the numeric keypad to enter a formula into a spreadsheet cell and forget to unshift the key to use the asterisk as a multiplication sign. The result is usually more irritating than harmful.

Some of these problems may be alleviated with creative macro programming. If the Esc key is too often pressed by mistake with disastrous consequences, its function may be swapped with that of another key in a less accessible area of the keyboard.

Straight key-swapping alone, however, will not solve the <PrtSc>/* problem, since the same two functions would then be present on another key. A better solution would be to define a macro for a different key to produce an asterisk.

POTENTIAL PROBLEMS

There are some common pitfalls with macros of which you should be aware:

- In most cases, macro definitions are temporary unless you explicitly save them. If you call a macro that is no longer defined, you may obtain undesired results.

- Loading macro files will usually overwrite all previously loaded macros unless you explicitly specify "merge" or "append." Change a macro's name so that you will not lose a macro you still want to use.

- When defining macros, be sure to request user input when input is required and to refer to the input variable when entering the command; otherwise, you may end up creating an endless loop.

- When naming macros, be sure the keystrokes you are defining are not already in use by your application for another function you want to retain; otherwise, the macro will take precedence, and the previous function will be disabled.

- Be sure that the keystrokes (**hot key**) that call up the macro utility menu are not also used by another resident utility. If there is a conflict, you must reassign the hot key in one of the utilities.

If you approach macro creation with caution, you will avoid these problems and discover some exciting solutions. The following descriptions of keyboard macro utilities provide a number of tools that allow you to determine what your keyboard can do for you.

THE UTILITIES

Keyboard macro utilities give you control over your keyboard whether you are operating at the DOS level or inside application programs. Over the years, new features have been added to these utilities, which go far beyond their original function of assigning your commands to specific keys. The features provided by these programs are discussed in the following order:

- Macro Definition
- Menus and Windows
- Macro Playback
- Key Swapping and Layout Definition
- Other Features

Macro Definition

Macros are defined by first selecting an **i.d.**, which is the key or key combination that will be used to execute the macro. With a few exceptions, any key in any "shift state," i.e., that key alone or in conjunction with <Shift>, <Ctrl>, or <Alt>, may be assigned a macro. Some macro utilities even allow you to assign macros to short words.

Then, you enter the definition. Macros may be several thousand characters in length. In general, the characters of text or the commands are entered exactly as they would have been typed if there was no macro; however, many features are offered to address special situations:

- fixed or variable-length variables

- pause commands for a fixed length of time or until a key is pressed

- GOTO commands to allow branching and looping

Many utilities also allow you to attach descriptive text to any macro. Such descriptions can be helpful since they will be more meaningful than the macro i.d. and perhaps easier to read than the commands themselves.

Macros frequently can be created "on the fly" from within an application program. This method is useful for adding macros to your library as their usefulness occurs to you or for creating temporary macros that are helpful for your current task only.

More frequently, macros will be stored in macro files for repeated use. Macro files can be created or edited in a number of ways:

- by an internal text editor that usually provides helpful prompts and automatically formats the macro file

- by any word processor that can produce straight ASCII files, as long as the user follows the required macro file format

- by "recording keystrokes" while entering the text or commands "on line" to actually perform the task

- by "recalling" previous keystrokes if the task was just recently performed (most of these utilities can recall characters stored in a buffer)

All of these macro utilities allow you to create nested macros several levels deep; that is, one macro may call another, which in turn calls another.

Most macro utilities come with a few predefined macro files. These predefined macros serve two purposes: they are good examples to learn from, and they tend to be very useful as they stand. Macros can be provided to enhance the operation of Lotus 1-2-3, dBASE, several word processors, and various printers.

Menus and Windows

All keyboard macro utilities can be used to build menu systems. At the very least, a macro can be created to display a menu. The menu choices then represent other macros or DOS batch files that call up your applications software and load its corresponding macro file.

Many macro utilities provide additional features to design pop-up windows and menus. These displays overlay part of your screen but do not clear the screen; therefore, the original display is still present when the window or menu is closed. This feature may be a separate utility or may simply be another command written as any other macro command.

With text windows, you can also build context-sensitive help systems for your menus, for DOS, as well as for your applications. With most macro utilities, long text may be composed from any word processor that can create ASCII files and then be incorporated into the macro.

Since macros can be nested, the menus or help text may begin with an index from which the user selects another menu or a specific topic.

Macro Playback

When macros are created from within an application program, they usually take effect immediately. Once several macros have been created, however, it is more useful to recall them from a macro file.

Once a macro file has been loaded, it remains in effect (in RAM) until it is explicitly shut off or is replaced with another macro file. For example, you would load a macro file associated with your word processing software when you start up the word processor. Then, when you leave word processing for your spreadsheet application, you would load your spreadsheet macro file, replacing the word processing macro file.

Several macro utilities include a feature that allows you to load two macro files at once, effectively adding the macros from the second file to the first, at least temporarily. This new merged file can be saved over one of the original files or as a new file.

All macro utilities include some facility for turning themselves off, allowing you to return to your original keyboard settings. This facility may include any combination of the following features:

- clear all macros from RAM
- clear one macro definition from RAM
- temporarily suspend all macros in RAM
- bypass a macro this time only

Key Swapping and Layout Definition

All keyboard macro utilities may be used to switch key codes from one key to another. At the very least, a key can be chosen to identify the macro and then can be defined as a different key; however, key-swapping and layout functions are often performed by an auxiliary program that is separate from the program used to define more elaborate macros.

Generally, when you call this facility, a diagram of the current keyboard settings will appear on your screen. You enter a key whose definition you want to change. That key blinks and/or is highlighted on the diagram. You then enter the key whose definition you want assigned to the first key. You can always change a key back to its original meaning by pressing it twice.

Key swapping works differently than other macro definitions in that the entire key, including its shift states, is swapped. For example, suppose you changed the PtrScr key to the letter "p." You would lose both the PrtSc and the asterisk function on that key, and you could type both an uppercase and lowercase "p" from that key.

Those utilities that provide layout features usually provide a few already defined, popular alternative layouts. These layouts may include the DVORAK configuration or layouts that more closely match popular brands of typewriters and/or other computer keyboards.

Layout programs work very closely with your computer's hardware; therefore, compatibility problems may arise if you are using a nonstandard clone or even a standard brand with a new, slightly deviant ROM chip. In case of incompatibility, you may need to use the general macro facility to reconfigure your keyboard layout.

Other Features

Many of these utilities have evolved over the years into multi-purpose programs, adding many ancillary features. Some of these extra features are keyboard-related and some are security-related.

Most keyboard macro utilities allow you to set the size of the **type-ahead buffer** beyond the number of characters prescribed by DOS. This buffer holds your keystrokes, while your computer is executing previous requests, until the computer is ready to process new input.

Several different security features are provided by these utilities. Each of the utilities described here provides one or more of the following features:

- protecting macros from being overwritten
- locking the keyboard or blanking the screen
- encrypting files

Note that, except for file encryption, these features provide very low levels of security.

User Interface

Most of these utilities may be either menu-driven or command-driven. Menus may be a preferable interface for learning the operations and for creating macros. Command modes allow the macros to be loaded and played back from batch files or from other macros.

The menus may be accessed at any time, even from within applications software. The applications software will stop processing while you are actively working with the macro utility and will resume when you exit the utility.

Compatibility

Keyboard macro utilities are all RAM-resident and take a fair amount of control of your computer's hardware and operating system while you are running applications software. For these reasons, they tend to have more compatibility problems with nonstandard hardware and "misbehaving" software than other utilities.

Most of the utilities provide a great deal of specific information in their manuals as well as "readme" files on incompatibilities. They explain what the effects are, why they occur, and what can be done, if anything, to make the macro utility work with particular hardware and software.

To minimize conflicts with applications software and with other RAM-resident utilities, the macro utilities frequently allow you to configure a number of settings:

- size of type-ahead buffer

- playback speed, i.e., speed at which the macro is "typed" into the application

- amount of RAM used by the macro utility

- graphics settings and use of screen-saver feature

- ability to change the keys used to call up the utility

Following are the specific features of each utility program.

PROKEY

RoseSoft, Inc.
P.O. Box 45880
Seattle, Washington 98145-0880
Telephone: (206) 282-0454

Software Features

Macro Definition

ProKey macros can be defined through the menu and text editor. Macros can be created on the fly by "recording" keystrokes and then be stored in files for future use. Once you have learned the macro file format, you can create macro files through any text editor that can produce ASCII files.

Macros can be assigned to almost any key in any Shift state. ProKey is one of the few macro utilities that also allows you to assign a macro to a multiple-character name.

Both fixed-length and variable-length fields may be included in any macro where you need to request user input. Fixed time delays from tenths of seconds to hundreds of hours may be written into a macro definition. A guard command is provided, which, if included in a macro definition, will prevent that macro from being erased when new macro files are loaded or when all macros are cleared from memory. Typing speeds can be set and changed within macro definitions.

Macros can be nested for an unlimited number of levels by ending each macro with a call to another macro. Looping macros can be created by ending a macro with a call to itself. ProKey will issue a warning if you try to define an infinite loop, that is, a loop with no variable through which you can instruct it to exit.

Macros also can be annotated with descriptions. Through the ProKey menu, you can view a macro file, complete with names, definitions, and/or descriptions.

ProKey provides several ready-made macros for popular applications software as well as a BASIC program that will create date macros.

Menus and Windows

ProKey's manual explains how to use the macro facility to build menus. A menu system in ProKey is a combination of macros and DOS batch files.

ProKey does not provide windows.

Macro Playback

Macros take effect immediately if they are created through the ProKey menu. Macro files may be loaded through the menu, from other macros, or through batch files.

Macro files in memory may be overwritten by or merged with subsequently loaded macro files.

You can interrupt ProKey's control at a number of levels:

- select access to a key's original definition just one time
- undefine one macro
- clear all macros from RAM
- turn off ProKey

Key Swapping and Layout Definition

LAYOUT.COM is ProKey's key-swapping program, which is run separately from ProKey. When LAYOUT.COM is called, two diagrams of your keyboard are displayed: the top half of the screen shows your original keyboard, and the bottom half shows the keyboard you are defining.

ProKey includes several predefined layouts, including three versions of the DVORAK layout and several computer keyboard layouts. These predefined files may be used as is or further modified to your specifications.

Other Features

ProKey may be installed in one-key typing mode so that Shift, Ctrl, and Alt key combinations may be entered sequentially. This mode can also be turned on and off through ProKey's menu.

ProKey allows the type-ahead buffer to be set to any number through the ProKey command line.

ProKey provides a screen-saver feature, which may be turned on or off through the command line.

RAM Management

The ProKey program takes up about 40K RAM. LAYOUT.COM is not loaded unless you explicitly call it up. The amount of memory ProKey reserves for macros may be set from 1K up to 30K bytes.

SMARTKEY

Software Research Technologies, Inc.
2130 S. Vermont Avenue
Los Angeles, California 90007
Telephone: (213) 737-7663
Sales: (800) 824-5537

Software Features

Macro Definition

SmartKey macros can be defined through the menu and text editor. Macros can be created on the fly by "recording" keystrokes and then stored in files for future use. Macros may also be recorded after the fact by recalling the commands in SmartKey's buffer, which holds the last 64 characters you have typed. Once you have learned the macro file format, you can also create macro files through any text editor that can produce ASCII files.

Macros can be assigned to almost any key in any Shift state. SmartKey offers a unique feature in its "Supershift" key. With this feature, the number of possible macros is just about doubled.

Both fixed-length and variable-length fields may be included in any macro where you need to request user input. Filter commands can control the input to be uppercase, lowercase, or numeric. The system date can be inserted automatically. Fixed time delays from one second to 255 hours may be written into a macro definition. Typing speeds can be set and changed within macro definitions.

Macros may be nested for an unlimited number of levels by ending each macro with a call to another macro. Looping macros may be created by ending a macro with a call to itself.

Macros can be annotated with descriptions. Through the SmartKey menu, you can view a macro file, complete with names, definitions, and/or descriptions. Macros can also be assigned short alpha codes as part of their descriptions. These "mnemonics" may be used in place of the macro name to play back the macro.

SmartKey provides several ready-made macros for popular applications software and printers as well as a sample menu system.

Menus and Windows

SmartKey has very sophisticated menu-definition and window-definition facilities. The menu and window commands are macro commands, which can be included in any macro file. Windows can be used alone to display messages or help text, or they can be used with menus to create a pop-up menu system.

Special window commands allow you to define the window size, position, colors, outline, and titles. Several windows can be defined to be displayed sequentially.

Macro Playback

Macros take effect immediately if they are created through the SmartKey menu. Macro files may be loaded through the menu, from other macros, or through batch files.

Macro files in memory may be overwritten by or merged with subsequently loaded macro files.

You can interrupt SmartKey's control at a number of levels:

- select access to a key's original definition just one time
- undefine one macro
- clear all macros from RAM
- unload SmartKey

Key Swapping and Layout Definition

PCKey.COM is SmartKey's key-swapping program, which is run separately from SmartKey. When PCKey.COM is called, a diagram of your keyboard is displayed. The altered keys will show their new definitions.

The layout is actually included in the PCKey.COM file. If you want to store more than one layout, copy the PCKey.COM file to a file of another name. SmartKey includes a predefined PCKey with a DVORAK layout.

Other Features

Through its menu, SmartKey provides access to many frequently used DOS functions. By accessing the SmartKey menu, these DOS operations may be run from within applications.

PCKey.COM allows you to expand the type-ahead buffer to 128 characters.

PCKey.COM may also be used to select one-key typing so that Shift, Ctrl, and Alt key combinations may be entered sequentially. You can select any combination of these keys to operate in one-key mode.

PCKey.COM provides a screen-saver feature that will blank the screen if the keyboard hasn't been touched in an interval, set by the user, of one to nine minutes.

PCKey.COM also includes a feature that will sound an audible click with every keystroke. This feature is useful for touch typists using silent keyboards.

Cryptor.COM is a separate file encryption program that can also permanently erase files so that unerase and restore utilities cannot recover those files.

SmartKey includes a keyboard-locking feature, which requests a three-character lock code to return the keyboard to a user's control.

RAM Management

The basic SmartKey program takes up about 21K RAM. PCKey.COM is not loaded unless you explicitly call it up. The amount of memory SmartKey reserves for macro definitions, windows, and help messages is additional, but may be controlled by the user.

In addition, both SmartKey and PCKey can be unloaded from RAM without rebooting your computer.

KEYWORKS

Alpha Software Corporation
30 B Street
Burlington, Massachusetts 01803
Telephone: (617) 229-2924

Software Features

Macro Definition

Keyworks macros may be defined through the menu and text editor. Keyworks' editor includes a sophisticated cut and paste feature. Macros can be created on the fly by "recording" keystrokes and then stored in files for future use. Macros can also be recorded after the fact by recalling the commands in Keywork's buffer, which holds the last 300 typed characters. Once you have learned the macro file format, you can create macro files through any text editor that can produce ASCII files.

Macros can be assigned to almost any key in any Shift state. Keyworks offers 245 additional special macro names consisting of the Alt key and a number from 10 through 255.

Both fixed-length and variable-length fields may be included in any macro where you need to request user input. The system time and date can be inserted automatically. Serial ports can be initialized from a macro. You can sound the computer's beep through macros. Fixed time delays from one to 65,000 seconds may be written into a macro definition. Typing speeds can be set and changed within macro definitions.

Macros may be nested up to twenty levels. When one macro is called by another, you are automatically returned to the first macro when the second has completed execution. A GOTO command, on the other hand, will not return control to the initial macro. Looping macros may be created by ending a macro with a call to itself. A warning message will be displayed if you define an infinite loop.

Macros can be annotated with descriptions. Through the Keyworks menu, you can view a macro file, complete with names and descriptions.

Keyworks provides several ready-made macros for popular applications software and printers, as well as a sample menu system.

Menus and Windows

Keyworks has very sophisticated menu- and window-definition facilities. The menu and window commands are macro commands that can be included in any macro file. Windows may be used to display messages or help text or pop-up bar menus.

Special window commands allow you to define the window size, position, colors, outline, and titles. Bar menus may be created so that a highlighted bar can move through the selections via the cursor controls. With this type of menu, you can choose to display macro descriptions rather than their keystroke i.d.'s to keep the menu as simple as possible.

Macro Playback

Macros take effect immediately if they are created through the Keyworks menu. Macro files can be loaded through the menu, from other macros, or through batch files.

Macro files in memory can be overwritten by or merged with subsequently loaded macro files.

You can interrupt Keywork's control at a number of levels:

- select access to a key's original definition just one time
- undefine one macro
- clear all macros from RAM
- suspend operation of Keyworks
- unload Keyworks from RAM

Key Swapping and Layout Definition

Keyworks has no separate key-swapping feature or layout configuration facility.

Other Features

Through its menu, Keyworks provides access to many frequently used DOS functions. By accessing the Keyworks menu, these DOS operations can be run from within applications.

Keyworks provides a screen-saver feature, which will blank the screen if the keyboard hasn't been touched in an interval, set by the user, of one to 999 seconds.

Keyworks has a file encryption feature, which can also permanently erase files so that unerase and restore utilities cannot recover those files.

Keyworks' cut and paste feature can be used outside of macro editing to move screen information within files, between files within an application, and between applications.

RAM Management

The minimum Keyworks configuration takes up about 64K RAM. The amount of memory Keyworks reserves for macro definitions may be controlled by the user.

In addition, Keyworks may be unloaded from RAM without rebooting your computer.

Other Software in this Category

SUPERKEY

Borland International
4585 Scotts Valley Drive
Scotts Valley, California 95066
Telephone: (800) 255-8008

UTILITIES I

IBM Personally Developed Software
PO Box 3280
Wallingford, Connecticut 06494-3280
Telephone: (800) 426-7279

RE/CALL

Yes Software Inc.
390-10991 Shellbridge Way
Richmond, B.C. Canada V6X 3C6
Telephone: (604) 270-4152

NEWKEY

FAB Software
PO Box 336
Wayland, Massachusetts 01778
Telephone: (617) 358-6357

CHAPTER 7

SPREADSHEET UTILITIES

Spreadsheet software has been credited with starting the microcomputer revolution. It is still one of the most commonly used microcomputer applications, and there is a great deal of competition in this category.

With software, as well as hardware, popularity feeds on itself; users want assurance of current and future compatibility and consistency so they can realize a return on their investment in training.

Developers of popular software often appear conservative in updating and expanding their software to include the latest shortcuts and features. The "after-market" takes up the slack. Users discover needs, create solutions, and market the solutions.

One measure of popularity is the number of books, magazine articles, and even entire monthly magazines devoted to a particular package. The user base must be large to support such publications.

Another indication of popularity is the number of related software products, which appear to supplement a specific application program, often providing shortcuts and additional features before the original developers do. These application-specific utilities are the subject of the following two chapters.

THE PROBLEM

Spreadsheet software is often used as a middle management tool. Detailed analytical iterations are performed on pages of data with complex interrelationships. The final output, however, is usually directed to clients and upper management; therefore, it must be clear, concise, and of presentation quality.

Most spreadsheet software offers an array of powerful functions to accommodate divergent needs; however, most spreadsheet software could be improved in the following areas:

- compatibility
- backup
- documentation
- data base presentation

Compatibility

Most computer users have found that one application software package cannot efficiently address all of their computing needs. Each type of application has particular strengths and weaknesses for dealing with particular computing tasks. Most computer users use two or three different applications, frequently performing different operations on the same information.

Spreadsheet software is often used to analyze data from another source, usually a mainframe or microcomputer data base application. Data transfer is, therefore, an important function, and compatibility between application files becomes an issue.

As new data base and spreadsheet software is released, the problem grows. New releases, with important new features, are often incompatible with previous versions of the same application.

Software developers provide several types of conversion facilities to deal with incompatibility between data files, including

- upgrade conversions
- specific popular conversions
- general ASCII conversions

When an upgraded version of a product is released, software developers usually provide for the previous user base. If data files are incompatible between two versions, the upgrade usually includes a separate conversion utility so older files can be used with the new software. Downward conversion utilities are not as common.

Some software developers realize that proprietary file formats work against them if they are trying to increase their user base; therefore, several application programs include translation facilities to and from other popular applications, either within the same application category or between different categories.

Many software developers recognize the value of importing and exporting data between different types of applications; however, since there are as many different file formats as there are programs in the marketplace, developers cannot afford to address every possible situation. In these cases, applications frequently provide a facility for importing and exporting ASCII files. This particular data format is standard enough to accommodate most situations in which compatibility is an issue.

The major problem with many conversion facilities is that you must structure the data to be converted. Several trials are often necessary to create a useable data file. Incompatibility is not easily resolved. Many data transfer operations require one, two, or three translations, if they are possible at all.

Backup

Backing up data files is important in any application, but it is a particularly sticky issue with spreadsheet software for several reasons. Most spreadsheet software works with worksheet files loaded entirely in RAM. Also, most spreadsheet use involves considerable time for setup, testing assumptions, and formatting output.

As you know, RAM is volatile. If the power accidentally goes off, if your computer freezes and requires rebooting because of a conflict, or if you inadvertently erase your worksheet or replace it with another file, your work disappears.

Most spreadsheet software programs allow you to save a current worksheet to a file without closing the file. Even this operation, however, requires that you constantly remember to take such precautions, which can break your concentration.

Another important backup issue to spreadsheet users is disk space. Worksheets can grow very large. In addition, each iteration of the "what if?" questions associated with spreadsheet software amounts to another worksheet.

The data, along with blank cells and formatting specifications, consume a large amount of disk space. The method your spreadsheet software uses to store this information can make a substantial difference.

Documentation and Debugging

Lack of documentation facilities is the most difficult aspect of using spreadsheet software. Worksheet output in numbers, text, and graphs is the result of formulas. The clarity of the output, more often than not, belies the complexity of the underlying assumptions.

Frequently, you (or, worse yet, someone else) will need to revise a particular worksheet. The formatted output usually provides no clues to the specific formulas within the cells or to which cells are dependent on others.

Most spreadsheet applications provide a facility for printing formulas, but this facility does not solve the entire problem.

Even in its most basic form, mathematical notation is not easy to understand. In spreadsheet applications, where most formulas refer to other cells containing other formulas, and where many mathematical functions require peculiar program-specific notation, the problem is compounded.

Also, most spreadsheet applications provide limited formatting options for printing formulas. One common format is a vertical listing of cell addresses and corresponding formulas, but this format does not provide a visual image of the cell's interrelationships. Another method — printing the spreadsheet with formulas displayed — generally cannot accommodate long, complex formulas.

Data Base Presentation

Spreadsheet software provides a great deal of flexibility for printing worksheets. While formatting, the data can be moved and changed in appearance. On the other hand, to use a spreadsheet program's data base functions, such as Sort, Look Up, Count, and so on, the worksheet data must be rigidly formatted. Blank rows are not allowed. Field names must appear in one cell directly above the first row.

Many computer users prefer the intuitive simplicity of spreadsheet software even for data base-type purposes. It is easier to see what you are working on in spreadsheet software than in most data base management software; however, because a spreadsheet application is not a sophisticated data base management tool, data base functions tend to be limited.

For these reasons, data base-type reporting is desirable, although difficult to use within spreadsheet software.

SPREADSHEET UTILITY STRATEGY

An overall approach to using spreadsheet software is beyond the scope of this book; however, the following section will cover strategies that make it easier to take advantage of the utilities described later in this chapter.

The following two areas are worth consideration:

- documentation via range-naming and labels
- data base setup in spreadsheet software

Documentation

As you know, formulas using words rather than cell addresses are easier to set up and understand when you review a spreadsheet. Many spreadsheet applications provide a facility for naming cells and ranges of cells. In Lotus 1-2-3, you would type

/Range/Name/Create/NAME/A1..D9

to give the name NAME to the range of cells from A1 to D9. If you then wanted to move the entire range to another area in the worksheet, for example, P1 through S9, you would enter

/Move/NAME/P1

and press

```
<return>
```

Range names can be used as shortcuts to specifying a cell or range of cells in a formula or command. If a named range is specified in a Lotus formula, the range name, rather than the cell address, is displayed in the control panel.

Lotus provides a lesser-known but useful method of assigning names to single cells. Frequently, your worksheet will be set up with a column of values, for example, B1 through B9, adjacent to a column of descriptive labels, for example, A1 through A9. With one command, each label can be assigned as a range name to its respective value:

```
/Range/Name/Labels/Right/A1..A9
```

The word "right" indicates that the cells to be named are each located one cell to the right of the label. "Left," "Down," and "Up" may also be used if the values are not to the right but to the left, below, or above the labels.

Cell-labeling is also used by some utilities that automatically document worksheets. Each cell is named not by its column and row address but by its column and row label.

For these reasons, it can be very useful to set up rows and columns of values with adjacent descriptive labels.

Data Bases

You have learned how useful data base-type features such as Sort and Query can be in spreadsheet software. The utilities described in the following sections offer additional data base features such as report-writing; however, there are a few simple (but strict) rules you must follow to take advantage of these features.

In data base terms, a spreadsheet **row** is the equivalent of a **record**. Each spreadsheet **column** contains data for a **field**. Field names are designated by labels in cells directly above the first record. The entire data base consists of the range from the leftmost field name (label) to the rightmost field in the last record.

Lotus 1-2-3 cannot recognize blank rows or divider lines between records or field names and the first record. Also, data for any given column or field must be exclusively labels or exclusively values. Formulas may be used in value fields.

Because of these restrictions, certain types of formatting are not allowed. In general, you must choose whether you want a worksheet to function primarily as a data base or primarily as a presentable analysis. If you need data base functions, you may have use for the report-writing utilities described in the following sections.

THE UTILITIES

The utilities described next work with Lotus 1-2-3. Many work with Symphony, and a few are useful with other spreadsheet software as well. Four categories of utilities are covered:

- conversion
- backup
- documentation and debugging
- report writing

Conversion

Generally, in addition to spreadsheet software, conversion utilities are useful with many categories of applications; however, data transfer is more likely to be a routine task with spreadsheet software than with the other applications.

Conversion utilities copy and translate data base files or ranges of spreadsheet data to create new files compatible with different programs. While some conversion utilities can translate formulas and formats from one spreadsheet package to another, most do not. Macros are rarely translated effectively, even between versions of the same program. Transferred data usually consist of rows and columns of text and numbers.

The major benefit of conversion utilities is the assistance provided to ensure that your source data is correctly formatted to produce the desired conversion.

Conversion utilities, by definition, are compatible with more programs than Lotus 1-2-3. Such utilities facilitate transfer of data files to or from several different spreadsheet programs and data base managers as well as between spreadsheet and data base management software.

Backup

Any of the programs described in Chapter 12, "Backup Utilities," can be used to back up worksheets, but other backup utilities are particularly useful to spreadsheet users.

One type of backup utility will automatically save a Lotus or Symphony worksheet to a disk file at specified time intervals while you manipulate the worksheet in RAM. This type of utility addresses the primary backup purpose: preventing data loss.

The other type of spreadsheet backup utility condenses data so the backup file takes up less disk space. These utilities generally work by structuring the information in a more efficient format and omitting unnecessary information.

Usually, files saved with compacting utilities must also be restored by the same utility to expand the data into its original format.

Documentation and Debugging

Several utilities provide substantial documentation and debugging capabilities for worksheets created with spreadsheet software. One such utility allows you to attach annotations to individual cells or ranges of cells or files. Other utilities provide an automatic range-naming feature that allows printed formulas to refer to variables with descriptive text rather than cell addresses.

Debugging features analyze and comment on the logical flow of a worksheet and point out potential errors such as circular references, formula references to blank or label cells, and so on.

All documentation utilities provide several options for screen displays and printed reports.

Report Writing

Report-writing utilities for spreadsheet software essentially apply data base features to a range of spreadsheet cells. While data in a worksheet may remain restricted by the spreadsheet's data base requirements, the formatted output does not.

Additional data base functions include multiple sort keys, multiple-level subtotals, data from multiple files, and enhanced page formatting.

The specific features of each utility program are described in the following sections.

THE SPREADSHEET AUDITOR

Computer Associates International, Inc.
2195 Fortune Drive
San Jose, California 95131
Telephone: (408) 942-1727

Software Features

The Spreadsheet Auditor provides documenting and analytical debugging for Lotus 1-2-3 and Symphony and provides a landscape printing utility for use with any text file.

The Auditor is a debugging tool that provides several diagnostic tests, display modes, and reports to analyze the logic of your worksheet.

The diagnostic tests check for formula references to blank cells and labels, circular references, unused ranges, overlapping ranges, identical formulas, and other likely errors. Interrelationships among cells can also be explored by user-defined queries.

Display modes include separately formatted windows, a formula display, and a symbolic map of the worksheet (by type of cell content).

All diagnostic test results for a range or the entire worksheet can be sent to the printer. Full print formatting options are provided.

A Cell Noter program allows you to attach textual annotations to worksheet cells from within Lotus, Symphony, or the Auditor or to any directories or file names displayed through the Lotus or Symphony command menu.

The Cell Noter links your worksheet with a separate file containing the notes. The notes remain attached to cells moved within a worksheet. By pressing a function key, you can enter, display, or edit notes for any cell in a pop-up window. Another function key turns the window off, and another highlights annotated cells.

Printing options include printing a single note, printing all notes, printing a list of cells with notes, or printing a combination of the note and worksheet display.

The Spreadsheet Auditor includes a Sideprint utility for printing, in landscape mode, its own reports, worksheet files, or any other text file. Five predefined fonts and a font generator are provided in addition to several other print formatting options.

CELL/MATE

Clarity Software Corporation
13276 Research Boulevard
Austin, Texas 78750
Telephone: (512) 331-5356

Software Features

Cell/Mate is a documentation and debugging utility for Lotus 1-2-3 and Symphony worksheets. A worksheet is loaded into Cell/Mate, which performs analysis from Symphony-like menus.

Cells are automatically named with user-specified row and column labels. Several options are available for labeling, such as using more than one cell, adding a prefix or suffix, or repeating labels. These settings can be saved in a separate Cell/Mate disk file.

Three types of documentation using labels or cell references are available for your choice of cell, row or column, range, or entire worksheet. The first type lists each formula. The second type lists each formula and the formula of each cell referenced in the formula. The third lists, for each cell, every other cell with a formula including that cell.

Other reports include detailed analyses of cells containing formulas or constants, of circular references, of named ranges and range references in formulas, of cell protection and display formats, and of worksheet settings.

Several formatting options are provided for printing analytical reports.

SOS

Goldata Computer Services, Inc.
2 Bryn Mawr Avenue
Bryn Mawr, Pennsylvania 19010
Telephone: (800) 432-3267

Software Features

SOS (Save Our Spreadsheet) is an automatic backup utility for Lotus 1-2-3 or Symphony.

By default, when a worksheet is loaded in RAM, SOS saves the worksheet at two-minute intervals to a standard Lotus or Symphony disk file named SOS.WKS (or with a more appropriate extension) in the current directory of the default drive.

Options include saving the worksheet by its original file name, saving the file to a different path, or changing the automatic time interval between saving worksheets.

SOS may be disabled or reenabled as long as it is RAM-resident.

NOTE-IT

Turner Hall Publishing
10201 Torre Avenue
Cupertino, California 95014
Telephone: (408) 253-9607

Software Features

Note-It is a documentation utility that allows you to attach textual annotations to as many as 100 Lotus 1-2-3 worksheet cells or to file names displayed through the Lotus command menu.

Note-It links your worksheet with a separate file containing the notes. The notes remain attached to cells moved within a worksheet.

Note-It is accessed by an < Alt/key > combination. By pressing a function key, you can enter, display, or edit notes for any cell in a pop-up window. Another function key turns the window off, and another highlights annotated cells.

Options include listing all cells with notes attached, searching through all notes for a particular character string, deleting a note, or printing notes.

Printing options include printing a single note or all notes, printing a list of cells with notes, or printing a combination of the note and worksheet display screen.

Cell note files may be converted to ASCII text files for further editing, printing, or combining into a worksheet file.

PC CONVERTER PLUS/REPORTS PLUS

Softsync, Inc.
162 Madison Avenue
New York, New York 10016
Telephone: (212) 685-2080

Software Features

Both of these utilities can be as useful for data base applications as for spreadsheet applications and can be used to integrate data bases with worksheets.

PC Converter Plus is a conversion utility. Data files can be converted from almost any data base or spreadsheet format to any other data base or spreadsheet format. Formulas and macros are not converted.

Much assistance is provided to ensure that your conversion is valid and to customize the new file to your specifications. For example, converting spreadsheet files requires providing range parameters. In the process, date field formats, field names and types, file names, and directory paths can be changed.

Reports Plus is a report writer and data query utility that can work with data files from almost any spreadsheet or data base software. As many as ten data files from different applications in different formats may be linked in the same report or query.

Each undertaking is a "task" in which a data file or files are selected, a selection query may be specified, and a report designed. In a file designation, field names and types may be changed without changing the underlying data file.

Queries allow record selection with any numerical, text, or date operators. Multiple and mixed conditions can be combined into one query.

Report options include field selection, calculated fields, column headings, page formatting, sorting, subtotaling, and counting.

Both utilities are menu-driven, and you are prompted for all information. All setups are displayed on the screen as they are created and may be saved for later use or modification.

Other Software in this Category

THE CAMBRIDGE SPREADSHEET ANALYST

SQZ!

Turner Hall Publishing
10201 Torre Avenue
Cupertino, California 95014
Telephone: (408) 253-9607

LOTUS 1-2-3 REPORT WRITER

Lotus Development Corporation
55 Cambridge Parkway
Cambridge, Massachusetts 02142
Telephone: (617) 253-9186

@LIBERTY

SoftLogic Solutions, Inc.
One Perimeter Road
Manchester, New Hampshire 03103
Telephone: (800) 272-9900

GRAPH-IN-THE-BOX

New England Software
Greenwich Office Park 3
Greenwich, Connecticut 06831
Telephone: (203) 625-0062

CHAPTER 8

DATA BASE UTILITIES

Application software is the mainstay of computer use. The most commonly used applications are those that serve a general purpose such as word processors, spreadsheet programs, and data base managers.

Data base management software, more than any other application, is frequently used at two distinct levels. The first level is as a relatively simple tool to store large amounts of similarly structured data for selective retrieval and summary analyses.

The second level is as a foundation for such important specific-purpose applications as general ledger accounting systems, sales order entry and inventory management systems, and customer, prospect, membership, or subscriber-tracking systems.

Due to the investment in specific-purpose application development and the volume and importance of stored historical data, product consistency, compatibility, and longevity are perhaps more significant to data base users than to users of any other applications.

As with the spreadsheet software discussed in the previous chapter, data base users creatively adapt their software to accommodate their needs for extra features and shortcuts.

Data base management software, and dBASE III in particular, is also the subject of many books, magazine articles, and several entire monthly magazines. Related software products keep appearing to supplement specific data base application programs. This chapter discusses in detail those data base-specific utilities.

THE PROBLEM

Instant and selective access to a large volume of data offers extraordinary analytical possibilities for any business or other information-gathering environment; however, new users quickly discover that a great deal of planning and data manipulation are required to realize all of that potential.

Ideas that may seem simple in theory can become complex in execution. Many data base management packages currently available for microcomputers are powerful enough to handle complex situations; however, many users do not want to devote so much time to learning and performing the required operations.

These data base applications suffer somewhat from trying to please everyone. The wide range of capabilities offered for the so-called power users raises expectations. But in trying to make these features easily accessible, the so-called user-friendly interface can be cumbersome and limiting.

Many users have requested relief from the following problems associated with data base management:

- slow data processing
- limited reporting functions
- repetitive complex programming
- slow command interpretation

Data Processing

It may take no time at all — just a one-word command — to ask a data base management program to sort a data base or locate a particular record. This one word, however, is interpreted into a complex algorithmic process by the software. The speed of the process itself is determined by the efficiency of the algorithm as well as by the processing speed of your computer.

Data base management software often seems to function spectacularly fast with relatively small data bases; however, as computer users become accustomed to data base operations and as computer hardware gains in capacity, data bases often grow quite large. Processing time deteriorates noticeably as the data base file grows.

Software developers have not concentrated as hard on increasing the speed of operations as they have on ease of use. They may provide alternate methods of performing an operation so that you can choose the method that is more efficient in your situation; however, tradeoffs must be made.

For example, dBASE III offers a FIND command and a LOCATE command. FIND takes an extremely short time to search for a record by the key field in an indexed data base file of any size; however, if you want to search by any field other than the key, you must use the LOCATE command. The LOCATE command executes a much longer process in any case, but the process is even longer with an indexed data base than with a nonindexed data base.

Sorting or searching through a large data base may take hours. This type of operation is a top candidate for the multi-tasking utilities described in Chapter 5 since you may have time to perform many other tasks while you wait.

Report Writing

The primary output users want from a data base is a report offering information in a list format. The data base may be sorted in a specific way; certain fields may be totaled; the records may be grouped; or only selected records and/or fields or summary information may be printed. But basically, the most common type of output requested is a listing.

All data base management software packages provide some fairly easy way to print out such a listing. The software varies a great deal, however, in the provision for sorting and grouping, computing fields, and selection and formatting options.

In dBASE III, for example, the REPORT function is a user-friendly, menu-driven facility for designing a report. Fields may be selected from more than one file, grouped, totaled, summarized, and formatted. Page formats include page headings, column headings, margins, and spacing.

However, for some users' purposes, many of these options are severely limited. Only two levels of subtotals are allowed. The column footers of "Subtotal" and "Subsubtotal" cannot be changed. All output is in a strictly vertical columnar format, e.g., subtotals can only be printed directly beneath their respective columns. There is no option for pausing for paper change. There is no facility for conditional printing, and so on.

On the other hand, just about anything you could conceive of printing, in any format, may be sent to the printer by writing a dBASE program rather than using the REPORT command.

Programming

The user interface for data base management software varies from package to package. Some provide user menus. Others operate via commands. Some offer a choice of either mode of operation.

If your software provides a command language, it may also provide for programming. Programming, in data base management software, generally consists of writing sequences of commands through a text editor and storing this **source code** in a text file. When you run the program, the commands are executed.

Not all data base management software provides for user programs. Those that do, however, offer virtually unlimited flexibility — if you want to invest the time and effort involved. There are three general reasons why you would want to write a program:

- to provide a shortcut for performing repetitive tasks

- to simplify a task or limit the options for a nonexpert user

- to perform a combination of operations not easily performed at the command level

Programs may contain only two or three command lines or several thousand command lines, depending on the magnitude of the task you want to accomplish. Even the simplest programs require some expertise in operating at the command level. Larger programs require more of that same expertise plus a great deal of analysis, planning, writing, and testing.

Command Interpretation

Powerful data base management software usually includes its own command language. The more closely a computer language resembles machine code, the lower level a language it is said to be. A data base management program's language is a high-level computer language. Its vocabulary and syntax are close to human language and, therefore, easy to learn. In addition, common but complex data base operations, such as SORT or TOTAL, are provided with one-word commands so that less programming is necessary.

Your computer does not understand this language, however, so the data base management software acts as an interpreter. Each command must be translated into machine instructions to be executed.

If you are working interactively with the data base management software at the command level, your computer may seem to respond immediately to each individual command you type in. But if you are running a data base command language program, your perception will be quite different. As the number of commands to be executed grows, the time it takes your computer to interpret those commands becomes more obvious.

DATA BASE STRATEGY

An overall approach to the use of data base management software is far beyond the scope of this book; however, this section will cover some strategies that will make it easier for you to take advantage of the utilities described later in this chapter.

The most useful approach to data base management involves following a principle of division of labor. You need to separate the following wide-ly disparate tasks:

- setting up the data base management system
- using the data base management system

This division of labor can be followed in a large organization, in a small business with an outside consultant, or even by one individual.

Frequently, the person with the technical expertise to set up the applica-tion is not going to be the person who performs the day-to-day opera-tions. A good programmer can set up an easy and secure system that a novice can run with very little training. In the case of just one in-dividual, it is still more efficient to design a complex data base system just once than it is to re-invent the wheel each time you need some in-formation.

You can learn a great deal from studying several sources:

- sample programs in your software manual
- programs generated by application generators
- advice in software compiler manuals

You will find that many data base management systems involve the fol-lowing modules:

- data entry
- viewing/editing data
- printing reports
- menus to tie the functions together

If most of your programs follow this format, you may find that after you have written and tested your first program, it can be used as a model for subsequent programs.

Assign file names logically so that it is easy to tell which files are related. Assigning similar file names to related files also makes some other operations, such as the following, easier:

- performing wildcard operations
- revising programs with Find and Replace routines

Speed can be captured or simulated by various means:

- When choosing among several possible methods, choose the method that will be fastest for the most common situation.

- Open files during screen-drawing operations; generally, a user will not grow impatient if there is some visible evidence of progress.

- For the same reason, periodically display the status of long operations, such as sorting or copying files.

- Group time-consuming operations that do not require user interaction so that the user may leave the computer to do something else during that time.

On the other hand, be sure to consider data security in conjunction with speed. Leaving files open unnecessarily increases the risk of data loss. Save memory variables whenever crucial variables change their values. Include avenues for safely exiting the system in as many places as possible.

If you know you are likely to use a compiler, read the compiler manual first for additional features, command restrictions, and programming suggestions. New and alternative features are almost always offered for the sake of improving performance; however, you should be aware that they represent differences between the compiler and the original data base management interpreter. Index files may not be compatible with both. Source code may not be compatible with both. Some of the most user-friendly interactive commands may not be translatable by compilers.

THE UTILITIES

All of the utilities described here work with dBASE III PLUS. Several work with other data base software as well. There are four categories of utilities covered:

- report writers
- application generators
- compilers
- templates

Report Writers

Report writers generally extend the user-friendly data base reporting function to include more complex operations and more flexible formatting. Frequently, their reports may be set up and run from within the data base application itself.

Additional features may include the ability to link several data base files for one report, group and subtotal at several levels, and define computed fields with more flexibility.

Additional formatting features may include graphics capabilities for line and box drawing, user-definable headers and footers, the option for text to appear at subtotal breaks, and facilities for easily entering printer control codes.

Report writer utilities may also incorporate alternative program routines that speed up some of the basic data base operations.

Application Generators

Application, in this context, does not mean the data base management software itself, but the system of command files and data file structures that fulfill a more specific purpose.

Application generators have evolved since programmers have experienced that many data base management systems are entirely comprised of similar elements, as mentioned earlier:

- data entry
- viewing/editing data
- printing reports
- menus to tie the functions together

With a relatively small and determinable number of specifications, an entire system can be designed that provides these basic elements.

Application generators are programs, usually written in a lower level language, that actually produce the data file structures and command language programs according to your specifications.

Application generators can produce a relatively complete system for a user without technical programming expertise. In addition, they can alleviate the need for repetitive complex programming for more expert users who are frequently designing systems.

These utilities generally take advantage of tried and true programming routines. Some application generator utilities may also incorporate alternative command algorithms to speed up some of the basic data base operations.

Compilers

Compilers translate programs written in high level languages into a low level language. In the context of this chapter, compilers translate data base command language programs into separate program files consisting of machine-readable code.

Compiled programs offer advantages over command language programs in the following areas:

- speed of execution
- security of program code
- freedom to run without additional software
- disk space required
- expanded features

Compiled programs run much faster than command language source code because all of the translation is already done. Compiled porgrams are executed without the time-consuming, line-by-line interpretation required for the source code.

Compiled programs are machine readable, but not easily read and understood by people. To study a program's logic, you usually need to examine the source code. To alter a compiled program, you generally need to alter the source code and recompile the program.

The machine-readable code, then, is effectively protected from unauthorized examination and alterations. Many application developers use compilers for the purpose of securing their program logic as well as for speeding up program execution.

Another advantage of compiled programs is that, in most cases, they may be run independently of the data base management software. This feature is not true of many of the so-called compilers that are packaged with data base management software.

The data files are usually compatible with both the compiled programs and the data base management software; therefore, it is often advantageous to have access to the data base management software in any case. The compiled programs may be used to run most day-to-day routines. But ad hoc projects will still require the data base management software.

Also, compiled programs usually take up much less disk space than source code. Combined with the ability to run independently of the data base management software, a great deal of disk space can be conserved.

Like the other types of utilities described here, many compilers incorporate alternative command algorithms and additional commands and features that speed up some of the basic data base operations. The differences between the compilers more often than not involve tradeoffs among speed, new features, and compatibility.

Templates

Templates are pre-written, specific-purpose applications, complete with data file structures and command files. Templates are generally written with the software itself in the software's command language.

Templates are available for many different types of software, but most often for spreadsheet and data base management software. Data base applications are particularly suitable for templates since it is common to divide the labor of designing a system and using it.

Data base templates are readily available, in compiled or source code form, as full-featured accounting systems, mailing list managers, and so on, for general or specific industry applications.

The following sections detail the specific features of several utility programs.

QUICKSILVER

WordTech Systems, Inc.
P.O. Box 1747
Orinda, California 94563
Telephone: (415) 254-0900

Software Features

Quicksilver is a full-featured compiler for dBASE III PLUS. This compiler is, if not the fastest, one of the most compatible compilers with dBASE III PLUS commands and data files.

Quicksilver expands on dBASE III PLUS's programming features by providing new functions and commands as well as "user-defined functions." Most notable among these enhancements is Quicksilver's windowing facility. Several commands are provided to create, keep track of, format, and fill pop-up windows.

Quicksilver does not support dBASE III PLUS's interactive full-screen commands like ASSIST, BROWSE, CREATE, MODIFY label or report, HELP, and so on. The noninteractive mode of these commands, where it exists, is supported. For example, APPEND BLANK and APPEND FROM are supported, but APPEND is not.

Quicksilver includes several helpful options for the compiling process itself. Compiling is a two- or three-step process, and each step is fully-automatic, i.e., once Quicksilver is given the first program's file name, all other related programs called from within the system are automatically retrieved and compiled.

The two-step process—compiling and linking program files—builds in automatic memory allocation to allow large programs to run partially loaded into RAM. At this level, low-level executable code may be run as is or debugged with Quicksilver's sophisticated debugging utility. The third, and optional, step is **performance optimization**, which, among other things, removes automatic memory management but produces native assembly code.

QUICKCODE PLUS/QUICKREPORT

Fox & Geller, Inc.
604 Market Street
Elmwood Park, New Jersey 07407
Telephone: (201)794-8883

Software Features

Quickcode Plus is an application generator for dBASE III PLUS. Standard Quickcode Plus applications may include over forty individual programs or procedures.

Multiple related data base files can be included in one application. Fields can be linked, computed, and/or validated in a number of ways. Multiple-page input and editing screens are available. Graphics features are provided for designing screens. Libraries of label and report formats can be included, along with printer controls.

Quickcode Plus offers such options as generating high-speed assembly language code for menus or generating menu programs in dBASE III code, and generating programs as separate program files or as procedures in a procedure file.

Quickreport is a relational report writer for dBASE II, III, and III PLUS. In this utility, reports may be full-page forms as well as tabular listings.

Enhanced dBASE report features include multiple linked files, up to 16 group breaks, record counts, and other statistical functions.

Formatting enhancements include suppressing repeated values, page footers, user-defined break headers and footers, formatting numbers, pauses between pages, and printer controls.

Quickreport includes a Runtime utility, which allows Quickreport reports to be run from the DOS prompt with neither the dBASE nor the Quickreport software.

The user interface for both of these utilities consists of Lotus-style menus and form-design screens. The two utilities can be used together or separately.

Other Software in this Category

CLIPPER

Nantucket, Inc.
5995 South Sepulveda Boulevard
Culver City, California 90230
Telephone: (213) 397-5469

FOXBASE +

Fox Software
27475 Holiday Lane
Perrysburg, Ohio 43551
Telephone: (419) 874-0162

FLASHCODE

The Software Bottling Company of New York
6600 Long Island Expressway
Maspeth, New York 11378
Telephone: (718) 458-3700

R&R

Concentric Data Systems, Inc.
18 Lyman Street
PO Box 4063
Westboro, Massachusetts 01581
Telephone: (617) 366-1122

SBT DATABASE ACCOUNTING LIBRARY

SBT Corporation
Three Harbor Drive
Sausalito, California 94965
Telephone: (415) 331-9900

CHAPTER 9

PRINTER UTILITIES

Printers are unique in the realm of microcomputer hardware. The variety of output choices and control methods is far greater than for any other computer peripheral.

Hundreds of different printers with widely divergent capabilities are available. They are categorized primarily by how they transfer ink to paper:

- daisy wheel (or thimble)
- dot matrix
- laser

Daisy wheel or thimble printers produce fully formed characters much like those produced by conventional typewriters. Printable characters are arranged on a disk-shaped daisy wheel or a cup-shaped thimble.

These printers print relatively slowly and noisily due to the mechanical processes involved in turning the print mechanism and generating each character's impact on the paper. Many improvements in speed and noise level have been made in recent years. Output speeds range from 10 to 100 characters per second.

The high-quality, fully formed characters produced by daisy wheel printers are similar to those produced by conventional typewriters. In sensitive areas, such as personal correspondence, many people will accept nothing other than typewriter-quality output.

Daisy wheel characters provide little room for flexibility. Only characters on the wheel can be printed; graphics are usually out of the question; however, wheels may be changed to provide different typefaces.

The relatively low-priced daisy wheel and thimble printers range from under $500 up to $2,000. Interchangeable wheels or thimbles cost between $20 and $50.

Dot matrix printers form characters with dots printed via pin impact on ribbon, thermal transfer, or ink jet. The choice of pins determining character form is controlled by software in the printer's ROM, removeable cartridges in the printer, and/or your computer.

Dot matrix printers print faster than daisy wheel printers because each character is formed "on the fly" from the same print head. Printing speed varies, even with the same printer, according to the mechanical and software methods used to define characters.

In general, higher-quality output requires more dots per character, which results in lower printing speeds. Customized characters formed by your software print more slowly than predefined characters. Printing speeds range from 15 characters per second for the near-letter-quality printing of low-end, dot matrix printers to several hundred characters per second for the draft quality of high-end printers.

Noise levels vary with the method of printing and the density of the dots. Ink jet and thermal transfer dot matrix printers tend to print more quietly than ribbon impact printers.

A wide range of quality is possible with characters formed from dots, even though dot matrix printing is usually associated derogatorily with computers; however, dot matrix printers can vary the number and arrangement of dots per character to produce high levels of quality.

Standard printheads come with 9, 18, or 24 pins. Generally, more pins generate higher-resolution printing; however, 9-pin printers can produce relatively high resolution with more than one pass per character.

Using dots to form characters provides a great deal of flexibility. Any character that can be designed can be printed, which is why dot matrix printers are widely used for graphics.

Dot matrix printer prices range from less than $300 to over $2,000, depending on speed and quality.

Laser printers use office copy machine technology to transfer images to paper via electrophotography. A laser scans a photosensitive belt, turning off and on to produce a photo image of the page to be printed. Toner is applied and selectively sticks to the light image. Paper picks up toner as it rolls over the belt. The laser is controlled by software in the printer's ROM, removeable cartridges in the printer, and/or your software.

Laser printers print faster than other printers, with output usually measured in pages per minute rather than characters per second. Available printing speeds range from 6 to 10 pages per minute, which, at worst, translates to several hundred characters per second.

As with dot matrix printers, complex, customized graphics and high-density characters can considerably slow printing speed. Like office copiers, however, laser printers can produce several copies of identical "originals" at high speeds.

Compared to daisy wheel and dot matrix printers, laser printers are virtually silent. More noise is generated by the mechanical sheet feeding process than by the printing itself.

Although laser printing resolution is still measured in dots, a typical laser printer offers 300 dots per inch, which often surpasses daisy wheel printing clarity.

Unlike printers that produce fully formed characters, however, laser graphics are completely flexible. The graphics capabilities of laser printers surpass those of dot matrix printers because of the higher resolution.

Laser printers are relatively inflexible in accepting different paper types. Paper-feeding mechanisms suffer from the same restrictions that apply to office copiers. Continuous-feed paper cannot be used, and acceptable sheet sizes are limited. Optional, add-on sheet-feeding hardware can provide additional flexibility.

Due to their complex technology, laser printers are the most expensive printers; however, prices have declined significantly since they were first introduced. Prices range from under $1,500 to over $10,000.

Clearly, many printer features are entirely controlled by software. Additonally, many of the more mechanical features may be positively influenced by the computer interface. Three aspects of printer performance will be addressed in this chapter:

- printer speed
- quality of output
- flexibility of output

Printer speed matters a great deal to computer users since the printer is the "bottleneck" of most computer operations. This situation exists because printers operate mechanically, not electronically like other parts of the computer. The quality and flexibility of the output matter as much to the people who recieve the output as they do to those who produce it.

The performance of the three printer types may be enhanced by one or more of the utilities described in this chapter.

THE PROBLEM

Each printer type offers diverse capabilities. Printers generally come equipped with a predefined character set of a given typeface and quality, usually including letters of the alphabet, numerals, and standard signs and symbols.

The character set and the features described in your printer's manual may reflect only a small portion of your printer's potential. Even the most flexible printers, however, must be properly instructed by software to perform their "tricks."

While many of your printer's features are accessed by software, it is often difficult to control such operations.

Printer Speed

Printer speed is determined at three points in the printing process:

- when your application software sends instructions to the printer

- when the printer reads and processes instructions

- during the printer's mechanical operations

Generally, you will direct a printer from within application software. Printing a data base report, a document, or a spreadsheet requires only that you select the application's print function.

The software then reads data from RAM or disk, processes it according to your specifications, checks if the printer is ready, and sends the output to the printer. The manner in which application software handles these procedures greatly affects the speed at which output is printed.

Some software, for example, will process your data one line at a time and check after each line is processed for an indication that the printer is ready for more output. If the printer is much slower than the application's processing, valuable processing time is wasted while you wait for the printer to request the next line. The reverse situation, in which application processing is slower than printing, can also slow both processes.

To a great extent, the mechanical capacity of a printer determines the printer's maximum speed. A printer's mechanical operations can be influenced by the type of printing requested of it. The less work required of the printer in a particular printing operation, the less time the printing will take. All print enhancements affect printing speed, including font selection, underlining, boldface, and graphics.

An obvious example is printing boldface characters. Your printer may perform this instruction by double-printing a line, producing boldface on the second pass, or it may print each character twice on the first pass. The single-pass method is always faster than the multiple-pass method; either way, additional printing must be performed to achieve the desired effect.

Print Quality

Print quality is primarily influenced by three factors:

- type of printer
- typeface or font
- print resolution

The quality of dot matrix printing varies greatly. Factors affecting print quality include the number of pins used to print dots, character design, and proximity of dots (or resolution). Generally, the more space between dots, i.e., the lower the resolution, the harder a character is to read.

Laser print quality is affected by many of the same factors as dot matrix print quality, but the range of resolution starts at a higher level. Letter-quality printers that produce fully formed characters do not usually present problems in print quality.

The choice of typeface, character design, or font is primarily subjective; however, some character designs are easier to read than others. Daisy wheels or thimbles with different typefaces can be purchased. Most dot matrix printers offer limited choices of predefined fonts. Laser printers offer more choices but often require that you purchase additional, expensive font cartridges or diskettes.

The clarity of dot matrix or laser printing can be enhanced by increasing resolution for any typeface. In dot matrix printing, such enhancement is usually performed through multiple passes over characters. In each pass, dots are repeated in a small increment to the left, right, above, or below each character. Most dot matrix and laser printers offer predefined codes to enhance print clarity.

Although many printers offer flexibility in choices of fonts and degrees of resolution, exercising the options can be difficult.

Flexibility

Printing effects are not limited to character design and degree of resolution. Other printing effects include

- printing special characters
- working around printer carriage width limitations
- filling preprinted forms
- special effects and graphics

Foreign language, mathematical, currency, and technical symbols present problems on any printer. Specialized fonts that provide a foreign language alphabet or scientific discipline's symbols may be available, but you are more likely to use these characters in conjunction with normal text than alone.

In this instance, your old typewriter offers some flexibility. On a typewriter, it is often possible to combine two characters to create a third character. For example, a lower case "c" and a forward slash can be combined to produce the cents symbol. Other characters, such as uncommon fractions, can be difficult to produce on a typewriter as well as on a computer.

Printing wide data base reports and spreadsheets may also present problems, even if you have a wide-carriage printer. For presentation purposes, you might design a report or worksheet to appear horizontally rather than vertically. Without special printing utilities, you have three options:

- condense printing as small as possible
- cut and paste, lining up columns side by side
- redesign, swapping vertical headings for horizontal headings

If the printer has a narrow carriage, you are even more restricted in print format. With a narrow carriage, inserting 8-1/2" × 11" paper horizontally isn't even an option.

Other printing effects may also seem easier with a typewriter than with a computer. For example, printing a single label or filling preprinted forms can be difficult to coordinate with a word processor. Lining up a label or form to predefined margins can be time-consuming.

You might need special printing effects, such as printing large characters, a logo, or other illustrations. While your graphics printer should accommodate such needs, they can be difficult to accomplish.

By accident, you may have found that strange combinations of control codes result in type fonts you might not otherwise have known your printer was capable of producing. With proper instructions, many printers can often produce type styles, character sizes, and graphics not mentioned in a printer's documentation.

If your printer's manual is not helpful, you must experiment with each possible code and combination to discover the printer's potential. If your printer's manual provides a great deal of information on how to define characters, you may still find that designing characters from scratch can be tricky and laborious.

The utilities described later in this chapter provide more convenient methods of releasing a printer's potential.

PRINTER STRATEGY

You can enhance a printer's performance by determining the tasks the printer is to perform, the instructions the printer needs to perform the tasks, and how the instructions can be relayed to the printer.

You can take several approaches in the areas of speed, quality, and flexibility.

Speed

Background printing can speed printing slowed by communication between an application and the printer. Some applications include background printing features that allow you to move on to other tasks in the application while printing is handled by another part of the program.

Even faster and more generally applicable are the DOS PRINT command, RAM-based and disk-based print spoolers, and hardware printer buffers, which all separate application processing from the printing. By using one or any combination of these techniques, separate processes can run at their respective, optimal speeds without interference.

You can also speed a printer's operation by lessening its workload. For example, you can print drafts of documents for proofreading or internal distribution in a "rough" mode without print enhancements and print final presentation copies in a slower, fancier mode.

You may be able to redefine some of your printer's routine procedures to print faster in enhanced modes. For example, if your dot matrix printer normally makes two passes over an entire line to enhance characters, you may be able to achieve the same effect in a single pass.

Also, you may be able to switch from unidirectional printing to bidirectional printing or change the printer margins. Time is saved if the print head can start each line without returning to the left of the carriage.

Print Quality and Flexibility

Quality and flexibility are determined by character definitions. Printers respond to control codes sent by software. Control codes can usually be defined as ASCII character combinations. Methods of sending instructions to the printer include

- using application installation modules to select a set of printer control codes

- sending ASCII instructions directly through an application's command language

- using programs external to an application

Application Installation Modules

The most common method of providing instructions to a printer is through application software. Since printers and printing instructions are notoriously nonstandardized, most application installation procedures include a Printer Selection module.

Many application programs handle the wide variety of possible printers in a relatively arcane manner. A diskette provided with the application package often includes a file or files containing separate instructions for each of a long list of possible printers.

While this method of finding and selecting your printer model consumes a great deal of disk space, it is extremely easy *if* your particular printer is listed. If, on the other hand, your printer is less popular or was introduced after the application software appeared on the market, this procedure can be difficult.

In the latter case, a printer's manual may suggest a compatible and popular printer more likely to be on your application software's list. If no compatible printer name is provided, you must experiment through trial and error.

Even more frustrating, however, is that the compatibility of the suggested printer might limit your printer's features. You might have purchased your printer because of special features, but application software may be unable to access those features.

For example, you might purchase an IBM graphics compatible printer that also prints in a near letter-quality mode, which you intend to use for word processing. If your printer is not included in the word processor's printer list, you can print by selecting the instructions for the IBM graphics printer; however, the IBM graphics printer includes no near letter-quality feature. You may be restricted to the limited capabilities of the substitute printer model.

Whether or not an application recognizes a particular printer model, it may provide no facility for selecting print features in its routine operations.

Data base management applications often print only single-spaced or double-spaced text and numbers in narrow-carriage or wide-carriage format, advancing to the next page when necessary. Word processing software requires these capabilities in addition to such print enhancements as bold, underlining, superscript, and subscript. Spreadsheet software requires the same capabilities as data base managers, but often requires additional graphics output.

If your application software handles a printer's basic requirements, it may not request for more input; however, with each of these applications (as well as with others), you may want additional print enhancements.

Application Command Language

Many general applications provide additional facilities to handle custom printing specifications.

The dBASE III PLUS command language, for example, can be used to send ASCII code sequences directly to the printer from the command mode, from within a program, or from within a report format. The following dBASE program instructs an Okidata Microline 192 or 193 printer to print in correspondence-quality mode:

```
* CORRESP.PRG
SET PRINT ON
??  CHR(027)+CHR(073)+CHR(003)
SET PRINT OFF
```

In this example, "SET PRINT ON" instructs dBASE to send subsequent output to the printer. The "??" command instructs dBASE to display the result of the following command without generating a subsequent line-feed. "CHR()" is the dBASE command to convert decimal codes to ASCII characters. The sequence "27,73,3" is the decimal version of the Okidata's correspondence-quality ASCII control code.

In Lotus 1-2-3 Release 2, printer control codes can be specified from the Print menu or embedded in cells to change print modes within a worksheet. The following Lotus commands instruct an Okidata Microline 192 or 193 printer to print in correspondence-quality mode:

```
/Print/Printer/Options/Setup\027\073\003
```

In this example, a printer **setup string** is defined to be issued when the worksheet is printed.

In WordStar Professional Release 3.3, four user-defined printer control codes can be defined through the WINSTALL custom installation program. The following selections define the WordStar command ^P^Q as an instruction for an Okidata Microline 192 or 193 printer to print in correspondence-quality mode:

D   Custom Installation of Printers

O   User-defined functions

User function #1   #027
                    #073
                    #003

Once defined, you can issue the WordStar command ^P^Q in any document to print in correspondence-quality mode.

In WordStar Professional Release 4, the same effect can be achieved by selecting Okidata Microline 192/3 from the installation program's Printer menu. This application defaults to printing in near letter-quality mode of any compatible printers listed.

You can also use control codes within these applications to achieve particular effects for a character, a word, a paragraph, or a report column.

External Programs

If application software provides no facility for issuing printer control codes, external programs can help accomplish the task.

You may, for example, write a BASIC program to run prior to your application. The following BASIC program instructs an Okidata Microline 192 or 193 printer to print in correspondence-quality mode:


```
10 REM corresp.bas
20 LPRINT CHR$(27);CHR$(73);CHR$(3);
30 SYSTEM
40 END
```

In this example, "LPRINT" instructs BASIC to send the subsequent command to the printer. The "SYSTEM" command exits the BASIC program and returns you to the DOS prompt.

When using this type of external program to send printer controls, be aware that your application software may not be "in harmony" with the printer.

Suppose you issue a control code to change your printer's line height so the output will be double-spaced. In this case, if the application is not aware of the change, the page numbering will not be synchronized. The page numbers will increment only every other page unless you adjust the page length in the application.

You might also need to change printer control codes within a document, for example, for a specific word or line. When using an external program, you might need to print portions of a document or report separately, exiting from the application to reset your printer.

Using a keyboard macro utility to define printer control codes can allow you to embed control codes in applications that do not otherwise provide this facility (see Chapter 6, "Keyboard Macro Utilities").

Alternatively, you may use application software to print a report to an ASCII file without print enhancements. You may then pass the ASCII file through an external program to add print enhancements.

The printer utilities described in the following sections provide many tools to help you achieve peak printer performance.

THE UTILITIES

Printer utilities unleash printer flexibility of which you may have been unaware. Given the variety of available printers, it shouldn't surprise you that a wide variety of printer utilities also exists. Many features are available for one or more types of printers, and many utilities offer a combination of features. Different printer utility features discussed next include

- print spoolers
- font enhancers
- landscape print utilities
- typewriter emulators
- special effects tools

Print Spoolers

Print spoolers may be RAM-based or disk-based. A spooler can receive data as fast as your application can send it, quickly freeing your application. The spooler then feeds data to the printer as fast as the printer can handle it, maximizing printer efficiency.

RAM-based spoolers set aside a portion of RAM to receive all data directed to the printer. **Disk-based spoolers** store data directed to the printer in temporary disk files to be sent to the printer. RAM-based spoolers are faster, but disk-based spoolers free more RAM for application software.

A disadvantage of hardware print buffers is that you may lose control of the printing process. For example, suppose your entire document has already passed from an application to the printer buffer when the printer jams. You will not be able to pause printing through your application software since the application thinks the printing is complete. When you fix the printer jam and reset the printer, however, printing will continue until the buffer is empty. This situation often takes more time to correct than the process saves in the first place.

Many software print spoolers provide extra control features to help you recover from such situations and continue. These features allow you to restart printing from a previous page, set priorities in the print que, or purge the print que.

Print spoolers can be effectively used with all three printer types.

Font Enhancers

Font enhancers send control codes to your printer. At a minimum, they can create compatibility between application software and an un-familiar printer. Used with imagination, they can assist you in creating a wide variety of characters, symbols, and alternative print enhance-ments.

Font enhancement utilities frequently include predefined control code sets for a variety of fonts and print enhancements for various printers. In addition, they usually provide facilities for defining your own control code combinations to achieve other effects. Some of these utilities work in a manner similar to those described in Chapter 6, "Keyboard Macro Utilities," i.e., they intercept and translate characters and codes on the way to the printer.

Although font enhancers provide the greatest benefits to dot matrix and laser printers, daisy wheel and thimble printers can also benefit from font enhancement features. Certain character definitions, such as com-bining two characters to produce a new one, can be used with any type of printer.

Individual font enhancement utilities exist for particular application software packages, particular types or models of printers, or for general use.

Landscape Print Utilities

Landscape print utilities solve the problem of constraint by printer car-riage width. Wide spreadsheets, data base reports, or any other docu-ments may be printed horizontally rather than vertically.

Landscape print utilities generally work from ASCII files generated by application software, i.e., you first direct an application to print its report to a disk file. The landscape print utility then reformats the file for the printer.

Frequently, landscape utilities include several font enhancement features to allow you to choose type styles, sizes, and other special effects for the final printing.

Landscape printing utilities work with dot matrix or laser printers. They cannot work with daisy wheel or thimble printers since they use the graphics mode to redefine all characters.

Typewriter Emulators

Typewriter emulators allow your computer to regress to the mechanical equivalent of a typewriter for occasions when a typewriter is easier to use. Such occasions may include

- filling preprinted forms
- printing one envelope or one label
- immediate testing of output
- sending control codes directly to the printer

Typewriter emulators work in one of two modes, usually offering the user a choice of

- one character at a time
- one line at a time

In the first mode, each key pressed results in a character being printed, just as with a typewriter. In the second mode, you can enter an entire line and edit it before pressing the Return key to print the line.

Special Effects Tools

This category of printer utilities consists of programs used to generate special graphics independently or in conjunction with your application software.

Features include the ability to

- design logos
- design graphics borders for pages of text
- design forms
- create large print for posters and signs

Specific features of each utility program are described in the following sections.

SIDEWAYS

Funk Software, Inc.
222 Third Street
Cambridge, Massachusetts 02142
Telephone: (617) 497-6339

Software Features

Sideways is a landscape printing utility for dot matrix printers. Originally created for use with Lotus 1-2-3, this utility may be used to print any ASCII file in landscape mode.

Global printing options include setting paper size, type style, type size, density, character and line spacing, and margins. Sideways recognizes and responds to most IBM and EPSON printer control codes embedded in text files. With Lotus 1-2-3 and Symphony, Sideways can specify different print options in different cell ranges.

Sideways can be run in menu or command mode. With Lotus 1-2-3, Sidways can print from within the application, so there is no need to create an intermediate print file. With Symphony, Sideways runs as an add-in application from the Symphony menu.

THE TYPEWRITER/SIGN DESIGNER/WIDESPREAD

Channelmark Corporation
Available from:

Power Up!
2929 Campus Drive
P.O. Box 7600
San Mateo, California 94403
Telephone: (800) 851-2917

Software Features

The Typewriter is a typewriter emulator that is run as an independent program. Entered text is displayed in the top half of the screen as you type; a function key menu is displayed in the bottom half of the screen. A ruler line across the middle of the screen displays tab settings.

You have a choice of printing each character as it is typed or printing one line at a time on either a dot matrix or daisy wheel or thimble printer. Additional features include adjustable margins and tab settings, word wrap, and form feed.

Sign Designer is another independent program that allows you to print large type (in landscape mode) on a dot matrix printer.

Each "sign" may contain up to ten lines. For each line, you can enter up to 122 characters of uppercase and lowercase text, choose one of three type styles, and select a character height up to 8 inches.

Print options include a choice of printers and printer ports, centering or left-justification, multiple copies, and high-density or faster printing modes.

Widespread is a landscape printing utility for dot matrix printers that can be used to print (in landscape mode) an ASCII file from any drive or subdirectory.

Print options include a choice of printers and printer ports, three type sizes, paper width, top and bottom margins, and multiple copies.

PRINTER BOSS

Connecticut Software Systems Corporation
30 Wilson Avenue
Rowayton, Connecticut 06853
Telephone: (203) 838-1844

Software Features

Printer Boss is a multi-purpose printer utility for dot matrix printers and includes a RAM print buffer, which is adjustable up to 32K bytes. The buffer may be turned on or off, and its contents may be purged from the main menu.

Several font-enhancing options are available with Printer Boss, depending on your printer's capabilities. First, you may select from your printer's default mode, a higher-quality (but slower), one-pass, double-density mode, or a two-pass, quad-density graphics mode. Three predefined type styles are provided within the two-pass mode. Several predefined font files can be selected or modified as needed.

If the printer is capable, you may select alternate character sets, character sizes, line spacing, margins, and other print options such as compressed, expanded, subscript, underline, and so on.

Printer Boss includes a landscape print utility, Sideline, that can print any ASCII file in landscape mode. If an application has no facility for printing to an ASCII file, Sideline can intercept data directed to the printer and create a print file directly from the application. Sideways includes seven fonts, in various sizes, that can be easily modified.

Printer Boss can function as a typewriter emulator, printing one line at a time. The input line can be edited before it is printed. Control codes can be sent directly to the printer in typewriter mode by entering a backslash followed by the decimal equivalent of the ASCII character.

Printer Boss includes a special drawing tool, Logoboss, to create and print graphic designs up to two square inches in area. Logoboss requires a graphics adaptor board. This utility includes facilities for drawing lines, boxes, circles, and ellipses. Short text strings can also be incorporated.

Setup configurations, font designs, and logos may be saved in disk files for subsequent use. Most functions are accessible by menu or in command mode, so Printer Boss can be run from a DOS batch file.

PRINTQ

Software Directions, Inc.
1572 Sussex Turnpike
Randolph, New Jersey 07869
Telephone: (201) 584-8466

Software Features

PrintQ is a RAM-resident, disk-based print spooler that allows full user control. All data directed to the printer is intercepted and queued in disk print files before being sent to the printer. At any time, even within an application, a status display can be called up for review and modification.

Several specifications can be defined to control printing. Hold prevents a print file from printing immediately. Priority determines when a print file will print in relation to other files in the queue. You may specify whether or not to automatically delete a print file after printing.

Form Alignment options include a pause before the first page or a pause before each page. Multiple copies and a nonstandard page length can be requested. A form name may be designated so that PrintQ will automatically group print files within the same priority designation requiring the same paper type.

If default specifications are used, queuing is transparent; otherwise, you may choose to be prompted for individual print file specifications each time a print operation is activated by an application, by the PrtSc key, or by an internal DOS command.

SMARTPRINT/INTERPRINTER

Software Research Technologies
2130 South Vermont Avenue
Los Angeles, California 90007
Telephone: (800) 824-5537

Software Features

SmartPrint translates ordinary keyboard characters and character combinations into printer control codes, allowing you to enter the defined characters in any application's data or document files to achieve desired printing effects. SmartPrint is most useful with applications that provide limited or no facilities for entering specific printer control codes.

InterPrinter is a similar utility program; its primary purpose is to translate control codes for one printer into those for another printer. InterPrinter is most useful with applications preconfigured to be compatible only with printers other than your own.

One or more translation pairs are saved in definition files, which can be created with any text editor that can produce ASCII files. SmartPrint is easy to use with SmartKey (see Chapter 6, "Keyboard Macro Utilities"), a keyboard macro utility from the same software developer.

Both utilities work with all types of printers. Of course, printer control codes are limited to those understood by your printer. Several predefined definition files for popular printers are provided with SmartPrint.

LASERWARE

SWFTE International, Ltd.
P.O. Box 219
Rockland, Delaware 19732
Telephone: (302) 658-1123

Software Features

LaserWare is a RAM-resident utility that provides print enhancement features specifically for the Hewlett-Packard LaserJet printer. LaserWare is most useful with applications not originally written for use with laser printers.

Text-formatting and font control options include all standard word-processing features as well as landscape mode, proportional spacing, mixing fonts, modifying fonts, line spacing, vertical and horizontal tabs, and table formatting. LaserWare includes several predefined "Profiles" for enhancing specific LaserJet font cartridges.

Graphics features allow you to use absolute and relative placement for vertical and horizontal lines of specified thicknesses, boxes, and shading. Graphics Capture can be used to merge screen graphics or graphics print files into any text file.

Paper-handling options include selecting from within a document the number of copies, feed option, paper type, and tray. With these features, options may vary from one page to another so that, for example, letters and envelopes can easily be printed together.

LaserWare provides a sophisticated macro system for defining frequently used commands. Also, LaserWare's "data" functions comprise a complete merge/print system that can accept data in several formats.

A "type-thru" option allows you to enter a text or command line directly to the printer.

PRINTKEY

NorthWest Software Associates
12469 East Olive
Spokane, Washington 99216
Telephone: (800) 422-6972

Software Features

PrintKey uses macros to translate ordinary keyboard characters or
character combinations into printer control codes. You may then enter
defined characters in any application's data or document files to achieve
the desired printing effects.

PrintKey's major asset is predefined macro files for over 100 daisy
wheel, thimble, dot matrix, and laser printers. Macro files can be easily
created or modified through the PrintKey menu.

PrintKey allows you to define print codes that can be entered into your
documents to be acted on as the document is printed and print codes to
immediately send instructions to the printer. PrintKey provides Pause
and Delay commands that can be inserted into any macro so you can
adjust the printer during print operations.

PrintKey also includes a RAM-based print spooler.

Other Software in this Category

PRINTSCREEN

DOMUS Software, Ltd.
303 Waverly Street
Ottowa, Ontario, Canada   K2P 0V9
Telephone: (613) 230-6285

FACELIFT 2

Companion Software, Inc., available from:

Sabre Systems Corp.
950 S. Bascom Avenue, Suite 1016
San Jose, California 95128
Telephone: (800) 255-8008

LETTRIX

Hammerlab Corporation
938 Chapel Street
New Haven, Connecticut 06510
Telephone: (800) 351-4500

FANCY FONT

SoftCraft, Inc.
16 North Carroll Street
Madison, Wisconsin 53703
Telephone: (800) 351-0500

TWIST & SHOUT

Intersecting Concepts
4573 Heatherglen Court
Moorpark, California 93021
Telephone: (800) 529-5073

CHAPTER 10

COMMUNICATIONS UTILITIES

The subject of microcomputer communications covers a lot of ground. Electronic mail, file transfer, networking, terminal emulation, and remote control are some of the diverse computer operations that involve more than one computer. Most of these operations can be performed with two or more microcomputers or with micros, minis, and mainframes.

Communications software is in itself a utility in the sense that communication supports the main applications for which you use your computer; however, many books are available on the major communication functions, and the general subject is too large and complex to be covered in this chapter.

Instead, this chapter will concentrate on more specific-purpose utilities that augment communication functions or provide special support to other applications.

THE PROBLEM

Much computer-to-computer communication goes on without trouble all the time; however, in every area there are some situations that cause frustration or require great expenditures of time and money. Some of these situations will be addressed here.

There are several reasons people communicate long distance through computers:

- to transfer specific data files

- to access the same computer system, programs, or data files on a routine basis

- to access another computer system for the purpose of monitoring its operations or altering the system

Data Transfer

Primarily through mainframe on-line data bases and electronic mail services, information is transferred routinely between microcomputers or between micro and mainframe computers. Many microcomputer users also use communications software for occasional transfers of data files between branch offices or between one business and its client.

Most of this information is transmitted in text form; therefore, the easy-to-use communications software is usually geared toward text or ASCII data. It may often be useful, however, to transmit a data file between two computers in non-ASCII form.

One prime example is transferring a Lotus worksheet from one branch office to another so that the receiver can make revisions and rerun the calculations. With an ASCII file transfer, only the text and numbers are transferred. The formulas are lost.

The most unfortunate aspect of this situation is that most communications software does not mention this limitation, and many users do not know that they must transmit binary files to rectify the problem.

Making matters worse, some communications software packages claim to transfer in binary mode rather than in ASCII. But the software actually performs intermediate translations as well so that ASCII data is transferred in binary mode. In this case, the original format is still lost.

If you want to transmit data in its original non-ASCII form, you should ascertain whether your communications software is capable of accomplishing this task and what settings you should use to assure that you achieve the desired result.

A related problem is the omnipresent issue of hardware and software incompatibility. Even if you are able to transmit a file in its original format, the computer on the other end may not be able to make use of it if it runs under a different operating system or with different applications software.

Networking

A typical hi-tech business scenario involves computer terminals on every desk, with several users accessing the same system and updating, looking up, or printing out data from the same source. Mainframes, and even minicomputers, set up expectations for this type of multi-user system.

The introduction of inexpensive microcomputers and inexpensive applications software made the computer age accessible to virtually all businesses when previously, only the largest businesses used computers; however, these microcomputers were "personal" computers, that is, single-user systems for the most part. While personal computers bring outstanding capabilities to a much wider user base, the idea of multi-user "networks" remains appealing in many situations.

Network systems and multi-user software are now becoming available for microcomputers. But most of these systems are expensive and complicated relative to the single-user computer's low cost and ease of use. For networking, new, expensive, and complicated hardware enhancements are often required. Usually, each workstation must be equipped with a full-featured computer and full-featured software. Often, the application software that employees have already learned must be completely rewritten or replaced.

So far, these facts have proven to be major barriers to networking in many businesses that have been most revolutionized by microcomputers. The businesses that are networking microcomputers are, more often than not, replacing or adding on to mainframe and minicomputer systems that were already in place.

Remote Access

There may be other times when you need occasional and flexible access to an off-site computer. Your requirements may be greater than simple file transfer, yet not routine enough to justify networking.

The most obvious of these situations is in software maintenance. An independent consultant or a member of the systems department in one location often needs to monitor some computer use, answer questions regarding a program's operation, or debug some software in another location. This type of situation has always required diagnosing the problem via telephone conversations, talking the user through the repair operations, sending off revised program files, and/or, as a last resort, scheduling a field trip.

There are many difficulties inherent in these methods of response. There may be dangerously incomplete messages or misreporting through verbal communication. Quick delivery methods and travel are expensive. In addition, delays until delivery or the on-site visit may cause intolerable downtime. During the field trip, you are likely to find you need some information you left behind, causing additional delays. At best, such occasions are highly inconvenient.

COMMUNICATIONS STRATEGY

An overall approach to microcomputer communications is far beyond the scope of this book. This section will, however, cover some strategies that will make it easier for you to take advantage of the utilities described later in this chapter.

Communication requires coordination. For example, one computer must initiate the call, and the other must answer the call. One method of coordinating the timing is to arrange for both computers to be attended by operators at the time of the call. This method generally necessitates some voice communication beforehand.

Another possibility is to set up and leave on line one or both computers for automatic, unattended communication at a later time. Many communication software programs include features for auto-dialing, auto-answering, and timed operations. In this case, it is also important to select a time when other important computer operations will not be interrupted.

Security considerations are important when leaving a computer on auto-answer and unattended. Be sure to take advantage of password facilities provided by the communications software. Standard password precautions should be taken. *Do not* choose obvious passwords; keep them private, and change them frequently.

Networking usually involves short-distance cabling rather than long-distance telephone line communication. Networked computers may be as close as different desks in the same office; however, many and more of the same aspects of coordination apply.

At least one server must be designated from all the computer equipment to be networked. Access to disk drives, printers, and other peripherals must be explicitly provided for each satellite or terminal. Each user must behave responsibly vis a vis other users in the network.

Networking requires a great deal of careful planning, whether you use a hardware-based or software-based networking facility. Ease of setup does not absolve the application software or the operator from a great deal more responsibility than is required for a single-user system.

The software-based networking utilities described in the following sections are considerably more accessible than hardware-based networks because they are easier and less expensive to set up; therefore, although a detailed networking strategy is also beyond the scope of this book, you should consider several stipulations:

- Application software must be specially configured to work properly and safely in a multi-user environment.

- Data files can never be safely accessed by more than one user or multi-tasking partition simultaneously without specially programmed file-locking, record-locking, and/or field-locking features.

- Certain computer operations, such as rebooting a linked computer or running backup, restore, or other disk maintenance utilities on a linked drive, should never be performed while a network is active.

- Software copyright laws apply to network environments in the same way they apply to multiple non-networked computers.

Be sure to read the warnings and suggestions in the network or multi-tasking software manual.

The following descriptions of remote access software may also be viewed as an alternative to expensive networking in certain situations. Although similar precautions should be taken, remote computing usually provides no security features other than password access. On the other hand, remote computing does not involve the most hazardous feature of concurrent multi-tasking.

Remote computing is limited to allowing one computer to monitor another's operations and to alternate control. Remote computing is easy and useful in the following situations:

- responding to occasional maintenance crises

- monitoring or reviewing someone else's computer operations

- running a full-featured microcomputer from a less expensive, more portable computer or terminal in an off-site location

THE UTILITIES

The utilities described here primarily address the followings issues:

- data file transfer
- software-based networking
- remote access

Data File Transfer

Virtually all communications software programs provide some method of file transfer. Many communication vehicles do not offer the ability to transmit data files directly and in unaltered binary format to and from any type of computer.

There are communication utilities, however, that allow for transmission of non-ASCII data over standard ASCII communication vehicles. These utilities convert the non-ASCII data to an encoded format of ASCII code before transmission and restore it to its original format on the other end.

This same method of operation is used by other utilities to allow transmission between otherwise incompatible hardware and software. These utilities are usually more specific in purpose and operation. The transmitting hardware and software and the receiving hardware and software must be specified. The conversion, which may occur before and/or after transmission, is tailored to the specific situation.

Software-Based Networking

As previously mentioned, software-based networking is often a relatively easy and inexpensive alternative to hardware-based networking. Entire books are devoted to the general concept of hardware-based networking; this chapter focuses on networking provided by software utilities.

The range of features offered by such utilities is wide and should be investigated according to your specific needs. Some provide the ability to transfer data and alternate exclusive use of limited peripherals, such as printers, modems, and hard disk drives.

Others offer a full complement of networking functions, allowing concurrent use of shared resources, regulating allocation, and providing security features.

Software-based networking utilities will not be automatically equipped with additional hardware enhancements such as extra serial ports, memory, and ROM-based security and other programs. These differences may somewhat limit their relative capabilities. On the other hand, you can usually obtain extra capacity by purchasing standard hardware equipment.

Remote Access

Remote computer processing, as provided by the utilities described in the following sections, is a relatively new concept for microcomputers. These utilities offer extremely flexible access to one computer by a remote computer or terminal. Once connected, the remote computer may perform any DOS functions, run, interrupt, and modify any software on the local computer from the remote keyboard, and view the results on the remote computer's display.

Generally, either computer can initiate the connection. The displays of both computers run in tandem. You can select which keyboard has operational control.

Additional essential features include password security, file transfers in either direction, remote printing capabilities, and the ability to tailor either side of the utility for different hardware such as modems, displays, and keyboards.

Following are descriptions of each utility program.

CARBON COPY PLUS

Meridian Technology
1101 Dove Street, Suite 120
Newport Beach, California 92660
Telephone: (714) 476-2224

Software Features

Carbon Copy is a communications utility that allows you to monitor or control one microcomputer from another microcomputer via a modem or cable connection.

Both computers must have the Carbon Copy software. One computer is designated as the local or host computer and the other as the remote computer. Either computer can initiate the connection, change settings, and process keyboard input. There is an option to disable remote keyboard input. The local computer must explicitly run Carbon Copy, so password control is only supplied for access to the remote computer.

There is a built-in, high-speed, file-transfer capability with data compression, encryption, and validation that works in either direction. A dialogue feature allows real-time text dialogue between the host and the remote operators. You may also switch the phone line between voice and data transmission.

Printing may be redirected from the host to the remote computer. A built-in conversion utility will translate printer control codes between popular printers. Screen images may be captured to a file by either computer and restored separately to the screen.

Another feature allows either user to perform DOS-type file functions on either computer by specifying the device. A call table is used to maintain names, associated telephone numbers, and passwords for auto-dialing.

Carbon Copy is offered as a stand-alone utility or with Carbon Copy PLUS, which combines the remote utility with several other popular file transfer protocols and host terminal emulations.

PCANYWHERE

Dynamic Microprocessor Associates, Inc.
545 Fifth Avenue
New York, New York 10017
Telephone: (212) 687-7115

Software Features

pcANYWHERE is a communications utility that allows you to run a microcomputer from any other computer or inexpensive terminal via a modem or a cable.

The pcANYWHERE software must reside on the host computer. The remote terminal can be just a terminal or another computer emulating a terminal. pcANYWHERE includes terminal emulator software for IBM PC's and compatibles. A limited keyboard macro facility will allow you to modify the remote terminal to be compatible with the host keyboard.

If the remote terminal is a computer, there is a built-in capability to transfer files in either direction with XMODEM protocol. Printing may be redirected from the host to the remote terminal if a serial printer is connected to the remote terminal. The terminal's BREAK key or equivalent key combination can be used to perform a soft reboot of the host computer.

pcANYWHERE may be run in nonresident, RAM-resident, or automatic mode. In resident mode, a hot key entered from the host computer activates the utility to either wait for the remote call or initiate the call. In automatic mode, the remote caller can call in at any time.

The pcANYWHERE setup routine includes an option to specify which keyboard the host computer will listen to—the host terminal, the remote terminal, or both. A password option allows you to specify up to 16 different passwords, each with their own automatically executed initial command line.

LANLINK/MULTILINK ADVANCED

The Software Link, Incorporated
8601 Dunwoody Place, NE, Suite 632
Atlanta, Georgia 30338
Telephone: (404) 998-0700

Software Features

LANLink is a software-based network utility. Without using expensive network hardware, one or more "satellite" computers, each with the LANLink satellite software, can be connected to a server computer with a serial cable between the computers' serial ports.

LANLink supports up to 16 satellites per server (if you have that many serial ports), but your computer's processing speed will probably limit the number of satellites long before this maximum is reached. Any computer may be both a satellite and server, with communications flowing in both directions through one cable. Use of the standard RS-232 serial port provides the ability to network remote computers via modem and telephone lines.

Standard networking features are provided, such as user i.d., password security, priority access, and selective peripheral sharing. The server can monitor each satellite's status from background partitions.

A disk-based print-spooling facility includes several control features, such as setting printing priorities, grouping tasks by paper-type requirements, sending printer control codes, selecting printers, restarting at specified page numbers, and saving or deleting print files.

LANLink incorporates MultiLink, a multi-tasking utility that offers user-definable processing priorities, memory management, concurrent processing, a full keyboard macro facility, and a bulletin board utility. Refer to Chapter 5, "Multi-Tasking Utilities," for a more detailed discussion of multi-tasking concepts.

By default, Alt/Function key combinations are used to switch between partitions, but most operations may be reassigned to other keys if they conflict with other software you use. Individual partitions may be automatically loaded with the desired applications via standard batch files—named AUTOEXE1.BAT, AUTOEXE2.BAT, and so on—to correspond with the partitions.

Resource sharing, including peripherals, directories, and files, can be tested for conflicting use manually or through batch files. Securer testing, testing within applications, and testing at lower than file level can only be performed by specially prepared multi-user software.

MultiLink Advanced includes all of MultiLink's features, enhanced for multiple users with the ability to use inexpensive "dumb" terminals to share the use of one computer. The terminals may be attached directly to the computer's serial ports via "null modem" cables or through modems.

MultiLink Advanced provides a disk-caching program, some color and graphics capability, and access to extended memory for compatible hardware and software.

LANLink and MultiLink Advanced can be used separately or together to create a network consisting of several computers and terminals.

ELECTRONIC ENVELOPE

McTel Inc.
Three Bala Plaza East, Suite 505
Bala Cynwyd, Pennsylvania 19004
Telephone: (215) 668-0983
Sales: (800) 628-3584

Software Features

Electronic Envelope is an easy-to-use utility that performs a single, useful function —allowing binary data to be transmitted through electronic mail systems that otherwise can transmit only ASCII data.

The one-line command, "INSERT filename newfile," will copy worksheets with formulas, documents with formatting codes, graphics files, and other non-ASCII files to a new specially coded format. The "newfile" may then be sent over electronic mail.

The one-line command, "REMOVE newfile filename," will copy the encoded file back to its original form. The Electronic Envelope utility must be available on both sides of the transmission.

Electronic Envelope contains a built-in validation routine that can be used to check if the REMOVE'd file matches the INSERT'd file.

One ancillary advantage to using this utility is that the transmitted file is effectively encrypted until the REMOVE command restores its original format.

MACLINKPLUS

Dataviz Inc.
16 Winfield Street
Norwalk, Connecticut 06855
Telephone: (203) 866-4944

Software Features

MacLinkPlus is a communications utility that provides for file transfer and translation between an Apple Macintosh computer and an IBM PC-compatible computer.

Without using expensive network hardware, a Macintosh and a PC, each with the MacLinkPlus software, can be connected with a cable between the computers' serial ports. MacLinkPlus will also work with a modem or network connection.

The translation facility will copy data files from PC application software, translating them into the data file formats of Macintosh application software or vice versa. For example, Multimate (PC) documents can be translated into MacWrite (Macintosh), or dBASE Mac data base files can be translated into files compatible with PC dBASE II or III.

Most popular word processing, spreadsheet, and data base manager formats may be read and written. Application software that is not included can usually import or export one or more of the formats that are provided. There is also a binary transfer option to transfer files without translation.

MacLinkPlus is run almost entirely from the Macintosh once the software has been set up on the PC. Note, however, that file translations and file transfers can be accomplished in either direction.

Other Software in this Category

REMOTE
TRANSPORTER

Crosstalk Communications

Available from:
Digital Communications Associates, Inc.
1000 Holcomb Woods Parkway
Roswell, Georgia 30076
Telephone: (800) 291-6393

RELAY GOLD
RELAY SILVER

VM Personal Computing Inc.
41 Kenosia Avenue
Danbury, Connecticut 06810
Telephone: (203) 798-3800

PC/PRIVACY

McTel, Inc.
Three Bala Plaza East, Suite 505
Bala Cynwyd, Pennsylvania 19004
Telephone: (215) 668-0983
Sales: (800) 628-3584

PRIVATE TALK

Glenco Engineering, Inc.
3920 Ridge Avenue
Arlington Heights, Illinois 60004
Telephone: (312) 392-2492

CHAPTER 11

DEVELOPERS' TOOLS

For those of you for whom no application software is quite good enough, you can develop your own. Many programming languages of various levels are widely used in developing applications for microcomputers.

Developers choose their programming language by several criteria:

- familiarity
- ease of use
- ability to accomplish the task at hand

Obviously, this last criterion is the most important. Most applications involve a variety of programming tasks, such as file management, screen operations, data sorting, and mathematical computations. A language that may excel in certain tasks may fall short in others. Although it might be possible to accomplish all necessary tasks in one language, it might be substantially faster and easier to accomplish some of them in another language. For example, low-level assembly language is extremely flexible and fast in execution; however, programming in assembly language is time-consuming and tedious. Many programmers find it more efficient to mix languages than to rely exclusively on one.

A programming language is nothing more than a set of rules regulating vocabulary, syntax, and structure in a computer program. A written program begins as an ASCII text file that follows those rules. It is the assemblers, compilers, and interpreters that translate these source code files into machine language on which your computer can act.

Many versions of compilers for the popular languages are available from various software developers. Each version supports a slightly different set of rules, tailored to enhance the language's flexibility and lighten the programmer's work load.

In addition many programmers take advantage of software libraries consisting of preprogrammed code, often in a lower-level language, for commonly required program routines. Such libraries can save a programmer hours of time re-inventing a wheel.

Many other programming "tools" are also available to ease the development process. Programming tools are generally software utilities that provide assistance, shortcuts, and enhanced capabilities to the developers writing the programs.

These tools may be available as utilities combined with a compiler or as separately packaged programs. Some are only useful with a specific compiler while others may function across languages. A few of the more general-purpose utilities that are available independently will be discussed in this chapter.

THE PROBLEM

There are several mechanical steps in program development, assuming the initial analysis is complete. In simple terms and in chronological order, a developer must perform the following steps:

- design input and output
- write source code
- compile, test, debug, and recompile

Designing Input and Output

Designing menus, input and output screens, windows, graphics, and reports is troublesome in most programming languages. Some of the most difficult elements include the following:

- screen visualization
- repetitive programming for input and output
- entry of graphics instruction in ASCII/decimal code

Recall that the more powerful data base management software includes full-screen report generators and, in some cases, a similar type of screen generator. A computer language and its compiler, however, do not constitute such a user-friendly application. Visualizing the screen may require manually assigning row and column locations to points on paper drawings.

This design must then be reduced to text that follows the vocabulary, syntax, and structural rules of the language. Input and output displays must be written separately since the vocabulary and, perhaps, the screen graphics will vary between the two functions.

Graphics may have to be described in some tedious way if the language provides no facility for graphics characters, repetitive commands, or mixing graphics with text and input and output variables.

Some higher level languages may include certain line and box drawing and screen clearing commands that simplify writing source code for the more standard graphics instructions.

Writing Source Code

A program starts out as a text file of source code. Such text files must be written in straight ASCII code to be compiled. Any text editor that can produce straight ASCII files can be used to compose the source code.

The DOS EDLIN program is such a text editor. EDLIN is actually, as its name implies, a line editor. There are no full screen capabilities. You cannot page back and forth with the cursor. If your file is too large to fit entirely in memory, you must explicitly write already edited lines back to disk and explicitly append new lines.

EDLIN does contain many advanced features for a line editor, such as Search and Replace, Move or Copy groups of lines, and function key editing assistance; however, in this age of sophisticated word processing, many people find line editors cumbersome to use.

Your word processor, on the other hand, is also a text editor that provides many fancy features. Editing text with a word processor is generally an easy task; however, word processors are geared toward formatting printed documents, not programs. Word processors provide no assistance in formatting structured source code.

Many of the standard word processing features, such as word wrapping, page breaks, soft carriage returns, hyphenation, and printer controls, get in the way of a programmer's source code. Even if the text looks clear in your word processing display, there may be non-ASCII control codes that are not displayed and will crash your program.

If your word processor has an ASCII format option, you can write and edit program source code in this mode; otherwise, you will need to use another text editor.

Debugging

Once the source code is written, it must be tested and debugged. Not only must the program run as intended, but the user interface and the resulting output must pass the scrutiny of the people for whom the program was developed. Rarely have all of these conditions occurred in the first run.

Most popular powerful programming languages are compiled into executable files in advance of being run rather than interpreted line by line when executed. This fact means that source code must be compiled, at least to a point, before it can actually be tested.

During the debugging stage, several problems may occur:

- a programming error may cause an endless loop

- a programming error may cause erroneous output

- the intended user may request a change in output format or processing logic

All of these possibilities make debugging a laborious process.

Locating programming errors, or even the precise spot to make a user's request for a change, is hard to do after the fact when there may be no clues to follow. Some changes may require a fair amount of trial and error.

The DOS DEBUG program is a tool for testing and debugging assembly programs. Its features include the ability to display, execute, and modify assembly language one instruction at a time and the ability to display and modify the contents of the computer's memory and processing registers. DEBUG is helpful if you can follow assembly language output, at least at the point where you have a problem.

Most likely, once you locate the instruction to be changed, you will want to change the source code. A change to the source code means that the source code must then be recompiled and retested.

PROGRAMMING STRATEGY

A substantial discussion of general programming strategy is far beyond the scope of this book. There are many different, and more or less rigorous, structured approaches to programming, all of which have proven their merits. On the other hand, the popularity of microcomputers provides programming access to many new users unschooled in these techniques.

There are several programming truisms that apply across the board:

- Up-front planning and approval saves work down the road.

- Modular programs are easier to debug and modify.

- Internally documented programs are easier to understand and modify.

Display screens and report output are *the* interfaces between the program and the user. They influence users' perceptions of ease of use, responsiveness, processing speed, accuracy, and general usefulness of your program; therefore, their design should be assigned a high priority. In all cases, designs for input screens and output displays and reports should be shown to the users for approval prior to committing them to code.

When you do begin writing source code, break up your application into modules, and document the purpose of each module and each set of instructions. Documentation is not so tedious if you learn to think "out loud" and enter your thoughts as you program.

Also, note that while comment lines will slow down the execution of interpreted programs, compilers will edit out the comment lines. In compiled languages, then, internal documentation will not cause any performance deterioration.

In interpreted programs, performance deterioration from comment lines can be minimized by placing commentary outside of loops or appending them to command lines where they will not be processed at all.

Maintain a disciplined formatting structure with consistent indentation, variable naming practices, and so on. This consistency will make it much easier to locate unbalanced commands and perform quick edits.

THE UTILITIES

The utilities described in this chapter are not the languages, compilers, and interpreters themselves, but tools that assist developers with program preparation. Presented in the order of use during the development process, the following types of utilities are covered:

- screen designers
- function libraries
- text editors
- debugging tools

Screen Designers

Screen designers can be used for designing input screens, output screens, and report formats. Typically, these utilities provide the visualization that is otherwise lacking. They allow you to "draw" your display directly onto the screen. Helpful features include full-screen editing capabilities, easy access to graphics characters, and the ability to print out the design or exhibit the display before you commit it to program code.

Screen generators will then actually write the source code in selected programming languages. Input and output variables can be defined and formatted. Additional programming can be included, such as a menu framework for the display screens.

The screen files may be edited and the programs regenerated. Or you can edit the generated programs themselves, incorporating them into larger program files or incorporating other commands into these programs.

Function Libraries

Other utilities that provide programming shortcuts consist of libraries of preprogrammed routines. These routines may be available in your programming language and can be compiled along with your source code. Or they may be available in lower-level languages as subroutines called from your programs.

Libraries will typically contain complex but commonly used functions, such as mathematical, statistical, or graphics routines. They will accept parameters passed from your programs if input is required.

Libraries can be purchased, or you can develop your own general-purpose routines. A single routine can be incorporated into your program, or you can link an entire library.

Text Editors

The text editing utilities designed for programming produce straight ASCII files. Rather than including the additional print formatting features of typical word processors, these text editors may include extra features designed specifically for programmers. They also tend to be less expensive than fully functional word processors.

The extra programming features may include checking for matching punctuation, automatic indenting, searching and replacing across files, command mode, and ASCII and hexadecimal arithmetic.

Debugging Tools

Debugging tools cover a broad variety of programs. The extra programming features of text editors may be considered debugging utilities. Many debugging tools come with their respective language compilers to assist in the development process.

Typical of these tools are **make** utilities. Make utilities allow you to keep track of related files. When one file is changed, the utility will realize that its related files must also be changed. Recompiling and re-linking can be performed more efficiently since only the affected files need be reprocessed.

Other debugging tools perform functions similar to the DOS DEBUG program; that is, they allow step or interruptable execution of a program. In between steps, they provide access to memory and CPU registers so that a programmer can monitor the program output each step of the way. In addition, if a problem occurs, the programmer can directly alter computer memory to provide a temporary fix and continue on with the testing process.

The following sections describe the specific features of each utility program.

DAN BRICKLIN'S DEMO PROGRAM

Software Garden, Inc.
P.O. Box 373
Newton Highlands, Massachusetts 02161
Telephone: (617) 332-2240

Software Features

Dan Bricklin's Demo Program is a development utility that allows you to create or capture, edit, and "run" a series of screen displays. Demo is particularly useful for designing input and output displays, presenting them for user feedback prior to programming, and/or demonstrating program operation for marketing or training. It can also be used to create user-directed or animated presentations for any purpose.

Display screens, or "slides," and overlays can be created from scratch on a full-screen blackboard will full editing capabilities. Editing selections for a character, marked block, or entire screen include background and foreground attributes, all displayable characters (with facilities for accessing special characters and attributes), repeat last character, and line and box drawings. A buffer can be created for characters entered at run time.

A separate "capture" utility can be run in resident mode and triggered by a Shift key combination to create slides from running programs. Macros may be "learned" to create editing shortcuts. A debug mode displays commands while you step through a set of slides.

You can name slides, define their order, and define the run-time mechanism that controls their flow, such as waiting for a specific key or period of time. Programmed actions for each slide may include sounding a tone, switching to the next, previous, or specific slide, or running another set of slides.

The slides may be outputted to a file to be run with the runtime program included, sent to a printer, or converted to a format acceptable to programming languages such as C and Pascal.

SCREEN SCULPTOR/FLASH-UP WINDOWS/SPEED SCREEN

The Software Bottling Company of New York
6600 Long Island Expressway
Maspeth, New York 11378
Telephone: (718) 458-3700

Software Features

These three utilities provide facilities for designing and generating program source code for screen displays and pop-up windows.

Both Screen Sculptor and Flash-Up Windows provide a full-screen blackboard will full editing capabilities. Editing selections for a character, marked block, or entire screen include background and foreground attributes, all displayable characters (with facilities for accessing special characters and attributes), repeat last character, and line and box drawings.

In Screen Sculptor, display screens can be created with input and output variable fields explicitly defined. Options include specifying input or display, the sequence in which variables will be read or written, the name, length, type, and number of decimal places, picture formats, and allowable range.

Source code in ASCII format may be generated in BASIC or Pascal. Options include generating just the code for one or more screen displays or adding lines to form a complete program. A list of errors that may have been discovered during program generation, such as duplicate or illegal variable names, can be displayed.

Flash-Up Windows can be used to create bar menus and pop-up windows. Window editing options include defining location and size, assigning help windows to particular menu choices, defining the response to a menu selection (commands, printer control codes, application input, etc.), and assigning keys to call the window.

Through the RAM-resident module, you can also capture screen displays to files that may later be edited and displayed like any screen you create.

This RAM-resident module also controls the display of windows from a window library, a captured screen image or a Screen Sculptor display via hot-key combination, assigned keys, the DOS command line or batch files, or from any programming or application command language.

Speed Screen is an add-on utility for these other utilities, which compresses screen definitions into a library that can be stored in RAM during normal computer operations. Using Speed Screen results in conservation of disk space and significantly faster screen displays.

HALO

Media Cybernetics, Inc.
8484 Georgia Avenue, Suite 200
Silver Spring, Maryland 20910
Telephone: (301) 495-3305

Software Features

Halo is a library of sophisticated graphics functions written efficiently in Assembler that can be easily incorporated into any program.

The library includes all standard functions such as lines, arcs, circles, ellipses, and polygons. Three text modes include several fonts for which the user can define height, line, and character width, interior fills, and angle of orientation. Graphic elements can be created interactively. Halo provides windowing and automatic clipping of images that surpass window borders.

The portability of the Halo routines is strengthened by absolute and relative addressing, alternate coordinate systems and conversion functions, and efficient file and data management systems.

Halo includes hardware device drivers for a wide variety of graphics boards, input devices, printers, plotters, and memory expansion boards so that the routines themselves do not need to be altered for changes in hardware.

Graphics displays may be modeled in memory to maximize resolution if your printer or plotter supports a higher resolution than your display adapter.

Separate libaries are available for separate programming languages. Halo supports various versions of many high-level computer languages, such as BASIC, C, FORTRAN, Pascal, Modula 2, and Lisp, as well as Assembler.

EC EDITOR

C Source, Inc.
12801 Frost Road
Kansas City, Missouri 64138
Telephone: (816) 353-8808

Software Features

EC Editor is a fast, full-screen, primarily command-driven text editor that includes several features useful to programmers. Only a selection of the many helpful features can be described here.

Standard editing features include insert and delete, block moves, and find and replace. Other features allow you to list all occurrences of a string within a range and back up a file being edited.

The DOS Interface allows you to execute at the DOS prompt any command from within the editor and to capture all DOS output to a buffer. For example, a directory can be listed right into the buffer, scrolled back and forth, incorporated into a file, and so on. Or you can view a compiler's error messages while editing your source code.

The buffer can be purged automatically on a first in, first out basis, or saved to disk. You can store a screen snapshot to a buffer. Deleted text is stored to a buffer and can be retrieved either through an Undo command or by opening a window on the buffer.

Up to five windows can be opened with different files and viewed simultaneously or viewed separately on the full screen. Blocks of text can be moved within a window or between windows.

Printer control codes can be entered directly. A printer translation file can be defined to your specifications. Printing can be spooled in the background. Several other print formatting options are also available.

A macro facility allows you to store command macros as Alt/function keys and text macros as Shift/function keys. Function key macros can be saved along with other configuration parameters in the EC Editor environment.

Explicit programmers' aids include the following:

- an on-line calculator that can perform arithmetic, ASCII, hexadecimal, binary, and octal base translations, and bit-wise operations

- tables of standard and extended ASCII codes

- C operators

- IBM extended keyboard codes

- auto-indenting and bracket-matching

- on-screen file comparisons

LATTICE TEXT MANAGEMENT UTILITIES

Lattice, Incorporated
2500 S. Highland Avenue
Lombard, Illinois 60148
Telephone: (312) 916-1600

Software Features

Text Management Utilities (TMU) consist of a collection of separate utilities that are helpful in editing source code program files. Several of these utilities have been adapted in function and form from the UNIX environment.

"Grep" will search through a set of files for a specified character sequence and print each line that contains a match. This function may also be incorporated into a C program to output a list of matches in, for example, an array.

"Splat" locates matching sequences of characters in a set of files in the same manner as Grep; however, Splat creates new files from the originals, operating on those characters according to the user's specification. Splat may be used to create a new file with global changes, such as search and delete, search and replace, or search and add characters.

Splat can be instructed to create the new version in a temporary file with a different file name extension or in a file of the same name in a separate specified directory, or Splat can overwrite the original file.

"Ed" is a line editor for text files. An optional automatic back-up feature is included. Standard line-editing features are also included so that text can be edited, appended, inserted, listed, joined, and so on. A block of lines can be moved; one file can be read into another; Search and Replace and other global commands can be executed on pattern matches or exceptions. The unique feature of Ed, however, is the ability to create script or command files to operate on one or more text files in batch mode.

"Diff" will display the differences between two files.

"Extract" can be used to produce a list of file names in a directory, with or without path specifiers and extensions, based on a file name specification with wildcard characters.

"Build" can be used to insert lines of text in a given file. When you enter the command to build a file, you can then input model lines to add structure and text to the lines from another file.

Extract and Build can be used together to construct DOS batch files.

"Wc" will display the count of characters, words, and lines in a file. A word is defined as a contiguous sequence of printable characters. Optionally, a checksum can be computed on a file to determine if it is identical to another file.

"Where" locates all executable files (COM, EXE, and BAT) with a given root file name along specified paths. The first file listed is the one that would execute if the command were given.

The "Files" utility allows you to perform across a number of directories DOS file operations on groups of files selected by file name specification, type of file, relative date, and/or relative size.

Special characters, such as a new line indicator, tab, space, backspace, escape, or a hexadecimal number, can be included in a character sequence by using special codes. Wildcard characters can be specified to generate a match on any single or group of characters in that place. A set or range of characters can be enclosed in brackets to indicate that any one of these characters should generate a positive match.

In most of these utilities, you can optionally ignore "white spaces," such as trailing blanks, ignore or strip out non-ASCII control characters, request all positive matches to a sequence of characters or all exceptions, and direct screen output to a file.

FAILSAFE

Princeton Software Group
Building B, Suite 283
301 North Harrison Street
Princeton, New Jersey 08544
Telephone: (609) 924-4463

Software Features

Failsafe is a memory-resident, menu-driven debugging tool, which is easy to use with any programming language. Failsafe may also be used simply to explore how your applications and other utilities work with memory and to experiment with specific memory locations.

At any time during your program's operation, you can temporarily stop it, examine and alter the contents of your memory, and continue. When "snooping" in memory, you can toggle between hexadecimal and character mode.

You can search in memory for a specific character string (delimited in quotes) or for a character's hexadecimal equivalent, or you may specify a specific memory location to examine.

One of Failsafe's most powerful features is its Unloop command, which allows you to break out of endless loops without rebooting your system and losing the contents of RAM.

Failsafe's ability to retrieve files from RAM also has many other potential uses, for example recovering from a disk-full error when writing a file within an application or recovering a BASIC program if you accidentally end it with a NEW command. In fact, there are specific menu options for automatic recovery procedures for WordStar and BASIC.

To retrieve data, you first specify a string to search for, cursor through the text, mark the beginning and the end of the string, and save it to a file name that you specify.

Other Software in this Category

PANEL PLUS

Lattice, Incorporated
2500 S. Highland Avenue
Lombard, Illinois 60148
Telephone: (312) 916-1600

WINDOW.LIB

Glenco Engineering Inc.
3920 Ridge Avenue
Arlington Heights, Illinois 60004
Telephone: (312) 392-2492

SAYWHAT?!

The Research Group
88 South Linden Avenue
South San Francisco, California 94080
Telephone: (415) 571-5019

SUPER-ED

Software Masters
6223 Carrollton Avenue
Indianapolis, Indiana 46220
Telephone: (317) 253-8088

PMAKER

Phoenix
Available from:

PC Brand
150 Fifth Avenue
New York, New York 10011-4311
Telephone: (212) 242-3600

CHAPTER 12

BACKUP UTILITIES

Backing up software, program files, and data files is one of the most important functions performed on a computer. Backing up primarily consists of maintaining copies of disk files on another disk, a floppy diskette, or other computer-readable media. If you need access to the copies because the original files have been damaged, altered, or are otherwise inaccessible, backup files are available.

THE PROBLEM

To determine the best method of maintaining backup files, you must first understand why you might need them. All information entered into a computer is vulnerable. Computers *can* make mistakes; people *do* make mistakes. Reasons for backup files include the following:

- damaged data due to bad sectors on the disk
- damaged data due to other computer hardware problems
- inaccurate data due to interrupted program flow
- inaccurate data due to input error
- need for previous versions of updated files
- long-term storage
- transferring programs or data between computers

Bad sectors on hard disks develop infrequently but not rarely enough. Bad sectors on floppy diskettes occur even less frequently, but they are not unheard of. For hard disks, remedies exist that prevent data from being written to a bad sector *after* the damage has been discovered (see Chapter 1, "Disk Maintenance Utilities"); however, data written to a bad sector before it is sealed off may not be recoverable. Programs written to bad sectors may not function properly.

Other hardware problems that may damage computer data are power surges, overheated components, and mechanical malfunctions.

Software programs and applications can cause erroneous data to be stored on the disk. An incorrect, inapplicable, or misplaced program instruction can interrupt a program's functioning. A hardware problem as simple as a printer paper jam can also interrupt the program flow. If a program's instructions are not executed in order or completely, the program's data files may be inaccurate.

User error contributes to the potential for incorrect or damaged data. Incorrect data might be entered in an application, and the program can proceed beyond the point where the error can be edited.

Turning off the computer, rebooting, or exiting an application without following necessary procedures can result in damaged or inconsistent data. Inadvertently erasing files, reformatting disks, or copying one file over another can also result in irretrievable information.

Even if malfunctions or mistakes don't occur, there are many reasons you might want to view a previous version of a file or files. For example, you might need to rerun an accounting report as of last month, or you might want to compose a new word processing document based on an earlier draft.

Backup files are also useful for long-term storage. If you want to clear your hard disk of information not currently important but also want to keep the information for archival purposes, you can store the files on diskettes.

Finally, copying a file or group of files to diskettes, as if you are backing them up, is often the most convenient way of transferring data and/or programs from one computer's hard disk to another.

METHODS

There are many ways of restoring lost data that may work, such as re-entering data or using file recovery utilities (see Chapter 1, "Disk Maintenance Utilities," and Chapter 2, "File Management Utilities"). Restoring recent back- up files, if they exist, is often the quickest, easiest, and surest solution.

If your original files are on floppy diskettes only, the best method of backing them up is to use the DOS COPY command to copy the files from one diskette to another. If you do not use subdirectories on your floppy diskettes, one command line will suffice. If subdirectories exist, the DOS DISKCOPY command can be used.

Backing up information on a hard disk, with its much greater capacity, presents the following problems:

- A full 20-megabyte hard disk fills over fifty 360K floppies.

- The number and size of the files result in a lengthy backup process.

- Files may individually occupy more space than a single floppy diskette; therefore, they cannot be copied with the DOS COPY command.

- The DOS COPY command can only reach files in one subdirectory at a time, so at least one COPY command line must be issued for each subdirectory.

- If the number and size of the files in any directory requires more than one diskette, separate COPY command lines must be issued for individual files or groups of files.

- File name specification is the only method of selection allowed with the COPY command.

Hard disk files can be backed up to floppy diskettes, a hard disk, or a tape drive device. Backing up to another hard disk or tape is one solution, but it requires the purchase and installation of expensive hardware.

DOS provides two utility programs, Backup and Restore, that allow you to perform the following procedures:

- Files that individually occupy more space than a floppy diskette can be copied.

- More than one subdirectory can be simultaneously accessed with one command line.

- Groups of files that require more than one diskette can be copied with one command line.

- File selection can be refined by directory date or archive bit.

Files backed up with DOS or any other backup program cannot be read directly from the backup diskettes by the standard DOS commands. They must first be "restored" using the associated Restore utility.

Utilities described in this chapter all improve on DOS in one or more areas, facilitating the process of backing up computer files from a hard disk to floppy diskettes.

BACKUP STRATEGY

The most obvious time to back up computer files is when the task of reentering the data would be more difficult than backing up and restoring files. If you use your computer on a daily basis, especially in business operations, routine backups are recommended.

You should maintain at least two complete **generations**, or sets, of backup files. In this way, if something goes wrong during the backup procedure, you can still use the previous generation.

If you do not discover erroneous data immediately after it is entered or damaged, the most recent generation may also be damaged. The more generations of backup files maintained, the more likely you will be able to restore accurate files.

After collecting the number of generations of backup files you intend to maintain, reuse diskettes of the earliest generation for the subsequent backup.

For example, assume you decide to maintain two generations. Label your earliest backup diskettes "A" and the next generation "B." The third time you perform a complete backup, you may reuse the diskettes labelled "A." The fourth time, you may reuse the diskettes labelled "B." The fifth time, use the "A" diskettes, and so on.

An efficient routine includes both complete and incremental backups of a hard disk. For example, you may decide to back up an entire hard disk once a week onto a single group of diskettes. On a daily basis, you may back up, onto different groups of diskettes, only files modified since the previous day. Determine the intervals between backups based on the extent of your computer use.

The directory entry for each computer file contains descriptive information that does not appear in the standard output of the DOS DIR command (See Chapter 2, "File Management Utilities"). One such piece of information is the **archive bit**. When a file is created or modified, the archive bit is set.

Most backup software can clear the archive bit to flag a file as backed up and read the archive bit to determine if the file has been created or modified since the archive bit was cleared.

Note that directory entries for files copied onto a hard disk with the DOS COPY command or renamed with the DOS RENAME command will not be updated as to archive bit, date, or time. Be aware that many software installation programs use the DOS COPY and RENAME commands within a batch file.

When determining files to include in an incremental backup, you may be tempted to rely on your memory of files you have edited. You should rely instead on the file date or archive bit to determine if a file has changed.

In many complex applications, changes or additions to one file will automatically update one or more other files. Even in the relatively straightforward use of spreadsheet or word processing software, you might update a general configuration file while working with a specific worksheet or document file.

Routinely backing up an entire hard disk is important for two reasons. First, if the need arises to restore all your files, restoring from one set of backup diskettes is quicker than restoring from several sets of incremental diskettes. Second, a full backup includes files added or modified by the DOS COPY and RENAME commands.

Documentation is an essential part of your backup routine. Label diskettes containing backup files with the date the backup was performed. Include a code (for example A, B, etc.) to identify the generation of backup files on the diskettes. Number the diskettes consecutively within a set. In addition, print for reference the names of backed-up files and directories.

Deviate from this routine if you suspect trouble. For example, if your hard disk is generating error messages, or if you insist on computing during an electrical storm, back up important files immediately. In this case, however, back up your files onto a fresh set of diskettes. If these files do turn out to be damaged, your routine backup generations should be intact.

When deviating from the routine, if you are using a backup utility that allows you to choose whether or not to reset the archive bit, *do not* reset it. The next routine incremental backup will then proceed as if there were no emergency backup.

After settling on a routine, save the option settings. Use software setup features or create a DOS batch file to further automate the procedure.

If you need to restore backup files in the case of damage to your current files, first cure the cause of the problem. Fix hardware problems, debug the program, or obtain correct information.

When the problem's cause has been eliminated, determine from backup documentation which set of backup files contains the files you want to restore. Be aware that if the data damage was caused by a hardware problem or unknown event, it is possible that damage not yet discovered has been simultaneously incurred by other files.

Before proceeding, carefully consider the order in which you restore backup files. Usually, you will restore first from the most recent backup diskettes. If you know when the damage occurred, restore from backup files created most recently before the damage.

If you don't know when the damage occurred, rerun your program after restoring the most recent backup files. If the problem still exists, restore from the second-most-recent backup diskettes. Keep testing and restoring until the problem on your hard disk no longer exists.

If you must restore a data file belonging to a complex application, be sure to restore all related files from a given backup set. As noted previously, many data files in a given application may be interrelated. Changes or additions to one file may automatically update one or more other files. If you restore only one data file, related files may not contain consistent data.

The easiest method of restoring from a set of backup files is to restore all those files. If you choose this option, be aware that perfectly good files that have been modified since the backup diskettes were created will be overwritten by any previous versions existing on the backup diskettes. Selectivity options in the backup software can assist you here.

Note also that some copy-protected software will not back up and restore properly through normal procedures. Refer to the manuals of copy-protected software for safe procedures. Selectively omitting offending files (usually hidden files) from the restore procedure will keep backup software from causing problems with copy-protected software.

THE UTILITIES

The programs described in this chapter back up computer files from a hard disk to floppy diskettes, improving on the DOS method in one or more of the following areas.

Speed

All utility programs covered in this section are faster than the DOS BACKUP and RESTORE programs. The restore function in nearly all backup software, DOS BACKUP included, is significantly slower than the Backup function; however, these utilities also restore files faster than DOS. Several factors enhance their performance:

- Multi-tasking is built into the programs so they can continue reading the hard disk (until DOS buffers are filled) while writing to a backup diskette. This task is performed by simultaneously using two DMA (Direct Memory Access) channels, which is allowed by most PC compatibles. For computers that do not allow this feature, it can be switched off, resulting in slower performance.

- Backup programs utilize their own special diskette formats, different from MS-DOS, that provide for more efficient placement of data on backup diskettes.

- These programs will format diskettes "on the fly," in contrast to the DOS BACKUP program, which must be interrupted and restarted if an insufficient number of diskettes have been formatted. One program, DSBACKUP, displays an estimate of the number of diskettes required for a specific selection of files. Faster results are achieved when you re-use diskettes already formatted with any of these programs' special formats.

- Some of these utilities take advantage of more than one diskette drive (or even more complicated hardware configurations) by backing up to different devices sequentially, which reduces time required to remove and insert diskettes.

- Some programs contain diskette sensors to recognize that you have inserted the next diskette, which eliminates the need for you to instruct the program to resume after a diskette switch. Since the diskette drive is never turned off, it resumes speed faster. A side effect of this feature is that you must switch diskettes while the drive light is on, which clashes with fundamental PC training.

Several other factors affect performance. The type and condition of hardware makes a difference. AT-compatibles are, of course, faster than PC-compatibles or XT-compatibles. High-density diskettes are faster, hold more data, and require fewer diskette changes than 360K diskettes.

More controllable factors include the sizes of subdirectories and individual files. The size of each subdirectory is more important than the size of individual files. A large number of small files takes longer to back up than fewer large files. The allocation of disk space to files will also affect speed (see Chapter 1, "Disk Maintenance Utilities"). The less scattered (in noncontiguous sectors) each file is, the faster a backup will proceed.

Selectivity

The DOS BACKUP command allows files to be selectively backed up by the following criteria:

- files with a directory date equal to or later than a specified date

- files modified (according to the archive bit of the directory entry) since the last backup

- files matching a standard DOS file specification; directory paths and wildcard characters may be used

For the most part, other backup utility programs duplicate and expand on DOS selectivity options. Additional features include the following options:

- using all arithmetic operators with the directory date, for example, < = (less than or equal to)

- selecting by type of file, such as hidden files

- an option to not reset the archive bit, which is useful for making more than one backup set of the same files

- listing more than one file specification for inclusion in the backup procedure

- using standard DOS file specifications to selectively exclude files

- displaying the list of files to be included in the backup according to the options selected

- selecting "on the fly" by displaying directory and file names and prompting for confirmation

DOS and other backup utilities allow you to add to an existing backup set without erasing files already on the backup diskettes.

Media and Format

As mentioned previously, these programs use their own special formats on standard diskettes. Most programs will work with both 360K and 1.2-megabyte diskettes and diskette drives, and some provide additional options.

In addition to increasing backup speed, special formats also increase the number of bytes that can be stored on one diskette. The software may compress data and/or write to smaller disk sectors; therefore, typically, fewer diskettes will be required if you use the format options.

For the most part, these formats are not compatible with DOS. While DOS cannot read files created by backup software, "compatible" formats at least allow a directory to be displayed. The special formats will produce error messages if you attempt to read the diskettes through DOS. These diskettes must be reformatted with DOS if you want to use them for reasons other than backing up files.

To allow backing up to DOS devices other than diskettes, e.g., another hard disk, some utility programs allow you to choose the DOS format, usually at the expense of speed and disk space.

User Interface

The DOS BACKUP program can only be accessed by entering a command line at the DOS prompt. In contrast, other utility programs offer some sort of menu interface to ease entry of backup and restore options.

Any of these programs, including DOS BACKUP, can be run from a DOS batch file. Other utility programs, however, offer further facilities for storing option settings and recalling stored settings for repeated use.

Some utilities also offer on-line help in the form of an on-line instruction manual or context-sensitive help messages.

Backup Documentation

Report output for all backup software is similar. To print a list of files backed up with the DOS BACKUP program, press <Ctrl/PrtSc> before typing the command line. The command line, the message to insert diskette number XX, and the names of files (with paths) are printed during the backup process. Pressing <Ctrl/PrtSc> at the end of the process stops the printout.

Other utility programs write similar information to a printer or to a file that can be printed with the DOS TYPE command. Writing to a file ensures that the backup process will not be slowed by your printer. Using print spooler software (see Chapter 9, "Printer Utilities") will also keep the printer from slowing the backup process.

Reports generated by these programs include additional information such as the backup diskette and sector number where each backup file is located and the time and date the backup was performed.

Restoring Files

As mentioned previously, the restore function is usually significantly slower than the backup function because writing to a hard disk must be done in the DOS format rather than the program's special format. Additionally, depending on the allocation of space on your hard disk, time may be consumed searching for available sectors to which to write the information.

The speed of the restore function is less important than the speed of the backup function since restoring files is more frequently a selective procedure. Fewer files are restored than are backed up.

When restoring files, in all cases, backup diskettes must be reinserted in consecutive order. When restoring all files in a backup set, you must start with diskette #1. When restoring only selected files, however, some utility programs allow you to start directly with the diskette containing the file or files you want to restore rather than forcing the computer to read all diskettes prior to the selected file or files.

Most programs allow selectivity in the restore function similar to that provided in the backup function. Paths and file names may be specified. Subdirectories will be recreated, if necessary. You may be allowed to skip files that have been modified since a backup, i.e., files whose archive bit has changed.

The major differences between the programs concern the method of selection. One method is to select a blanket option when you run the restore function. Another method is to answer a prompt before restoring certain files, and still another is to restore on a file-by-file basis. The utility programs discussed in this chapter offer different combinations of these methods.

Data Verification

The DOS VERIFY switch can be used with these programs to test if data just written can be read. In the utility programs, this option can be selected when running the program. The DOS VERIFY option slows the backup process considerably.

Some utility programs offer another verify function in addition to the switch provided by DOS. Such verify functions tend to run faster and, in contrast to DOS, actually compare written files to files initially read.

Specific features of each utility program are described in the following sections.

BACKUP MASTER

Intersecting Concepts, Inc.
4573 Heatherglen Court
Moorpark, California 93021
Telephone: (805) 529-5073

Software Features

Speed

Backup Master is the fastest of the backup utility programs tested. It is also the only reviewed backup utility that restores files almost as fast as it backs them up.

Backup Master tests your computer's DMA through its Setup Menu to determine if the program can use multi-tasking to operate at peak efficiency. If the test fails, you are instructed to reboot the computer and select DMA Slow on the Setup Menu.

Backup Master offers a proprietary diskette format that you may or may not choose to use. This special format allows faster backup and more efficient diskette space utilization. Diskettes may be formatted with the special format during the backup process. For fastest results, select FORMAT IF NEEDED on the Setup Menu. Peak performance is achieved when you reuse specially formatted diskettes.

If you choose to use diskettes without the special format, you must have sufficient DOS-formatted disk space available before running the backup function. Since you can run DOS commands from the Main menu, even disk formatting can be performed without leaving Backup Master.

Alternatively, you can use the nonformatting mode to back up your files to a specified path, another hard disk, or another DOS device.

Backup Master can take full advantage of two diskette drives (or even more complicated hardware configurations) by sequentially backing up to different devices.

Backup Master monitors the disk drive to stabilize motor speed and to recognize when you insert the next diskette, so you don't need to instruct the program to resume after a diskette switch. The diskette drive light stays on, but a screen prompt tells you when it is safe to change diskettes.

Selectivity

Backup Master provides unique file selection options for the backup and restore functions. The program allows files to be selectively backed up according to the following criteria:

- files modified (according to the archive bit of the directory entry) since the last backup.

- files that match a standard DOS file specification; directory paths and wildcard characters can be used.

The program also allows

- listing more than one file specification for inclusion in the backup procedure.

- using standard DOS file specifications to selectively exclude files.

- displaying the list of files to be included in the backup according to the options selected.

You also have an option to not reset the archive bit after backing up selected files.

Media and Format

Backup Master uses its own special format on standard 360K or 1.2-megabyte diskettes. The program can also back up files without its special format to any other DOS device, such as another hard disk.

In addition to increasing backup speed, the special format also increases the number of bytes that can be stored on one diskette. 400K fit on a standard 360K diskette and 1.3 megabytes fit on a standard 1.2-megabyte diskette; therefore, fewer diskettes are required than with most other backup utility programs.

User Interface

Backup Master may be accessed as a menu-based program or through batch command files. In the menu mode, the various levels of menus pop up fast in overlapping windows. From the menu, you may set up and run the program, preview the directories (with selected files marked), save setup files, and temporarily access most DOS functions.

On-line help is also available through the menu interface. Help screens are context-sensitive; the part of the help file that pops up when called is related to the menu currently displayed. The entire Help file can be scanned by scrolling with the cursor keys. As a straight ASCII text file, the Help file can also be customized.

Batch command files can be created to automate subsequent backups and restorations by using one of three methods:

- Through the menu mode, set up the selections as you want them recorded and select SAVE SETUP TO DISK.

- Through the menu mode, select RECORD KEYSTROKES and run through the steps of your backup operation, which allows you to perform separate backup routines with one command line.

- Edit one of these command files or create one from scratch with any text processor that can produce straight ASCII files.

A command file is then run from the DOS prompt by typing

`BM @filename`

STARTUP.BM is the name reserved for the default setup file. You can change this file's contents in the same way you save any setup file. To run Backup Master from the DOS prompt with the default settings, type

`BM 20`

The "2" selects the PERFORM BACKUP or PERFORM RESTORE option, and the "0" returns you to the DOS prompt.

Backup Documentation

Report output for Backup Master is stored in the history file. The history file is named with the date of the backup followed by the letter "A" if it is the first file created for that date, "B" if it is the second, and so on. The file extension is .HIS.

The history file can be printed after the backup by using the DOS TYPE command and pressing <Ctrl/PrtSc>. The heading of the report includes the date and time of the backup and a summary of program settings for include, exclude, and archive. Following the heading is a tree-type listing of paths, file names, and the location of each file by diskette and sector.

Restoring Files

The restore function in Backup Master provides the same include and exclude options as the backup function. Additional selection options include the following:

- Overwriting files of the same name in the same path. You can choose to always overwrite, never overwrite, or only overwrite files older (according to the directory date and time) than corresponding backup files.

- Restoring to original subdirectories (recreating them if necessary) or restoring to the default path.

When restoring only selected files, Backup Master allows you to proceed directly to the diskette with the file or files you want to restore rather than forcing the computer to read all diskettes prior to the selected file or files.

Data Verification

Backup Master provides a write verify option from the Setup Menu. This option performs differently depending on the media used for back-up files.

If you use an MS-DOS device, verifying with Backup Master is similar to the operation of the DOS VERIFY switch, i.e., data is read after it is written, but it is not compared to the original data. As with the DOS VERIFY switch, this selection may considerably slow backup or restoration processes.

If you use specially formatted diskettes, however, Backup Master reads and compares data it has just written.

DSBACKUP +

Design Software, Inc.
1275 W. Roosevelt Road
West Chicago, Illinois 60185
Telephone: (312) 231-2225

Software Features

Speed

DSBACKUP+ is actually two programs. DSBACKUP itself is significantly faster than the DOS BACKUP program but not as fast as other utility programs; however, it is considerably flexible. The companion program, Speedbak, is less flexible but ranks among the fastest programs tested. Both programs exhibit a high discrepancy between backup and restoration speeds.

Speedbak uses the multi-tasking capabilities of PCs with compatible DMA. No test is provided to determine whether or not your PC is compatible, but incompatible machines are listed in an addendum to the manual. An option has been added to run the program without dual-channel Direct Memory Access.

Speedbak uses its own proprietary format. The program formats while writing to a diskette not previously used with Speedbak. Fastest results are achieved, of course, when you reuse diskettes already formatted with Speedbak's special format.

DSBACKUP uses the standard DOS format. DSBACKUP can also format on the fly, although in a different manner than programs using special formats. A path to the DOS file FORMAT.COM is specified in the menu. When the program is ready for a new diskette, the menu displays options to continue the backup, format a diskette, or cancel the backup.

Speedbak can take advantage of more than two diskette drives by sequentially backing up to the different drives. DSBACKUP can back up files consecutively to any number and kind of DOS devices, including virtual volumes on mainframe computers.

Speedbak monitors diskette drives to maintain drive motor speed and to recognize when the next diskette has been inserted, which eliminates the need for you to instruct the program to resume after a diskette switch, as is necessary with DSBACKUP. A side effect of Speedbak's diskette sensor is that the drive light stays on; the screen displays a prompt when a new diskette should be inserted.

Selectivity

DSBACKUP and Speedbak excel in file selection. DSBACKUP allows files to be selectively backed up

- by date, using all arithmetic operators with the directory date, for example, < = (less than or equal to).

- by type of file, such as hidden or archive.

- when files match a standard DOS file specification; directory paths and wildcard characters may be used.

The program also allows you to

- list more than one file specification for inclusion in the backup procedure.

- display a list of files to be included in the backup under the current setting.

- select on the fly by displaying directory names and prompting for confirmation.

You also have an option to not reset the archive bit after backing up selected files.

Speedbak allows the same selection criteria as DSBACKUP except by date.

Media and Format

Speedbak uses its own special format on standard 360K or 1.2-megabyte diskettes. DSBACKUP can use the DOS FORMAT command to format same-size standard diskettes, but it can also back up files, without formatting, to any other DOS device such as another hard disk.

Both DSBACKUP and Speedbak store data more efficiently on backup diskettes than the DOS Backup program. In addition, DSBACKUP offers further data compression through its Squeeze option, usually without a decrease in backup speed.

DSBACKUP is the only utility program reviewed that provides an estimate of the number of diskettes required to hold a given selection of files. Regrettably, this feature is not available with DSBACKUP's Squeeze option.

User Interface

Both DSBACKUP and Speedbak can be accessed as menu-based programs or in command-line format. From the menu, you can set up and run the program and preview the selected files.

On-line help is available through the menu interface and even on the command line. Help screens are context-sensitive; the part of the Help file that pops up when called is related to the menu currently displayed. The entire Help file can be scanned by scrolling with the space bar.

Setup files can be saved through the menu interface under different file names and loaded to repeat a particular procedure.

All menu options, including loading a setup file, may be entered from the command line.

Backup Documentation

Report output for DSBACKUP and Speedbak can be sent to a file or printer. This was the only backup utility reviewed that includes the printer option from within the program; however, a print spooler is recommended to avoid slowing the processing (see Chapter 9, "Printer Utilities"). A report can also be run directly from the backup diskettes after the backup, using the included REPORT.EXE program.

The report is a tree-type listing of the paths, file names, and diskette number for each file.

Restoring Files

Restore functions in DSBACKUP and Speedbak provide most of the same file specification options as the Backup function. Date and file type selections are not available.

Data Verification

Both DSBACKUP and Speedbak provide a verify option from the menu. This option simultaneously performs two functions. The DOS verify function reads data after it is written. Additionally, the option checks that the sector written on the backup or restored disk duplicates the sector from which it is written. As with the DOS VERIFY switch, this selection may considerably slow backup or restoration processes.

FASTBACK

Fifth Generation Systems
7942 Picardy Avenue, Suite B-350
Baton Rouge, Louisiana 70809
Telephone: (504) 767-0075
Sales: (800) 225-2775

Software Features

Speed

FASTBACK has only one operational mode, but it is fast. This program is among the faster backup programs tested. Its restore function can take more than twice as long as its backup function, but restoration speed also ranked high among the tested products.

FASTBACK tests your PC's Direct Memory Access during the installation procedure to determine whether multi-tasking is compatible. If not, you are instructed to reboot your computer and run another installation program that reconfigures the software for slower processing.

FASTBACK uses only its own special diskette format. Diskettes not previously used with FASTBACK are formatted while files are being written to them, which slows the backup procedure. Even while formatting, however, FASTBACK is considerably faster than the DOS BACK-UP program. Fastest results are achieved, of course, when you reuse specially formatted diskettes.

FASTBACK takes full advantage of two diskette drives. The program will automatically back up the second drive when the diskette in the first drive becomes full and switch back to the first drive when the diskette in the second drive becomes full. In this way, manually removing and inserting diskettes doesn't slow the backup process. FASTBACK labels the diskettes to ensure that one diskette is not written to twice in the same backup session.

FASTBACK monitors diskette drives to maintain motor speed and to recognize that a diskette is in place. There is no need to touch the keyboard during the backup process. The diskette drive light stays on, but a screen prompt tells you when it is safe to change diskettes.

Selectivity

FASTBACK allows the files to be selectively backed up by the following criteria:

- files modified (according to the archive bit of the directory entry) since the last backup

- files that match a standard DOS file specification; directory paths and wildcard characters may be used

Subdirectories of the selected path may be included or excluded. You also have an option to not reset the archive bit after backing up selected files.

Media and Format

FASTBACK works with both 360K and 1.2-megabyte diskettes and diskette drives. One option allows 360K diskettes to be backed up using a high-density drive but readable by Frestore (FASTBACK's restore program) from a 360K drive. Another option backs up 720K of information on a 360K diskette in a high-density drive.

FASTBACK's proprietary format allows more data to fit on each diskette than does the DOS BACKUP program.

User Interface

FASTBACK can be run in three modes: interactive, command line, or command file. The backup program uses no menus, but the restore function does.

When FASTBACK is run in the interactive mode, five questions appear on the screen. Pressing the Return key after each line, i.e., accepting the default answers, results in a backup of the entire hard disk.

Without viewing the questions, the same answers can be entered in the command line used to invoke the program from the DOS prompt. This mode resembles the DOS BACKUP program.

The most flexible method of operating FASTBACK is through the use of command files. Each line in the file is identical to the command line mode, except the file doesn't begin with the word FASTBACK. This mode allows different drives, directories, and files to be grouped into a single backup set. The command file is run from the DOS prompt by entering

FASTBACK @filename.ext

Backup Documentation

Report output for FASTBACK is written to a file named FASTBACK.CAT. The catalog file is updated each time you perform a partial backup. It is re-created from scratch each time you perform a full backup of your hard disk.

The file can be printed after the backup by using the DOS TYPE command and pressing <Ctrl/PrtSc>. The information includes a label code, date, and time of the backup set, which is followed by a line for each file including file name and path, directory date and time, backup diskette number, and location on the diskette.

Restoring Files

FASTBACK's restore program is named Frestore. Running Frestore displays a menu from which files can be selected. Files can be restored one at a time, or you can start the restoration process at any file and allow the program to continue until you stop it. No provision is made for wildcard file specifications.

You can choose, as blanket options, to replace all existing files or skip files that exist on the hard disk. Alternatively, you can choose to be prompted for confirmation before replacing each file that already exists.

Data Verification

The DOS VERIFY switch can be used by adding "/v" to the command line, but Frestore offers a better alternative with its own verify function.

The Frestore verify function compares backup files on diskettes to files on the hard disk. As with the restore procedure, files can be verified one at a time, or the procedure may be started from any file and continued until you stop it.

If a comparison error is found, perhaps because of damage to the diskette since the backup, data on the backup diskette will be reconstructed. The program can accommodate up to one error per track on each diskette. No other backup utility program reviewed offers this reconstruction feature.

Other Software in this Category

BACK-IT

Gazelle Systems
42 North University Avenue, #10
Provo, Utah 84601
Telephone: (800) 233-0383

INTELLIGENT BACKUP

Software Laboratories, Inc.
202 East Airport Drive, #280
San Bernardino, California 92408
Telephone: (714) 889-0226

BAKUP

Software Integration, Inc.
9800 South Sepulveda Boulevard, #310
Los Angeles, California 90045
Telephone: (213) 776-3404

CHAPTER 13

MISCELLANEOUS UTILITIES

It is not surprising that utilities can be difficult to categorize or that the categories overlap. This chapter describes several utilities not previously discussed in this book.

DESKTOP ACCESSORIES

Desktop accessory utilities typically run in RAM-resident pop-up windows to provide instant access and the ability to use their features in conjunction with your application software. Features may include calculators, calendars, alarm clocks, telephone/address directories, automatic dialers, and notepads.

Desktop accessories are frequently combined with other general-purpose utilities and hardware products. One reason these utilities are combined is to alleviate RAM-conflict problems. If you have no need for these other utilities, you might want a stand-alone desktop accessory product.

SIDEKICK

Borland International
4585 Scotts Valley Drive
Scotts Valley, California 95066
Telephone: (800) 255-8008

Software Features

SideKick is a RAM-resident utility of pop-up windows that can be accessed from within most application software.

The monthly calendar is initially set for the current date, but it can be scrolled forward or backward a month or year at a time over decades. A datebook is attached that "explodes" an appointment page for each day.

The full-featured calculator performs standard arithmetic functions with calculator-type memory as well as conversions among decimal, hexidecimal, and binary bases. An ASCII table displays characters with decimal and hexadecimal equivalents.

The telephone directory is an ASCII data base for names, addresses, and telephone numbers created with Notepad or other software. The autodialer can find a telephone number in the telephone directory or anywhere on the display screen and automatically dial a telephone through your modem.

The notepad is actually an ASCII text editor with many advanced word processing features. Each note can be several pages long. You can cut and paste between notes or from your application's display screen and perform other block operations. Notepad provides optional, automatic time and date note-stamping.

Other Software in this Category

SPOTLIGHT

Lotus Development Corporation
55 Cambridge Parkway
Cambridge, Massachusetts 02142
Telephone: (617) 253-9186

GEM DESKTOP

Digital Research, Inc.
60 Garden Court
Monterey, California 93942
Telephone: (408) 649-3896

CONVERSION UTILITIES

Compatibility has been an issue ever since the second computer was manufactured. Technological advances, a lack of standards, competition, proprietary techniques, and different user preferences all contribute to the problem of incompatibility.

Compatibility, as it relates to transferring data files between different software programs and between computers via modems, has already been discussed in Chapters 7 and 10 on spreadsheet and communications utilities. The utilities described in the following section address compatibility as it relates to different disk operating systems and formats.

Conversion utilities allow you to perform file operations on a diskette with a foreign format. You can copy files from one disk format to another, read a foreign diskette's directory, erase files, and even format diskettes in the foreign format.

Generally, these utilities are available in several formats, each compatible with a different type of "host" computer, i.e., the computer from which the utility will be run.

MEDIA MASTER

Intersecting Concepts, Inc.
4573 Heatherglen Court
Moorpark, California 93021
Telephone: (805) 529-5073

Software Features

Media Master reads from, writes to, and formats disks in any of several PC-DOS, MS-DOS, and CP/M formats. Data may be transferred from foreign formats to a host format on another diskette or directly to a hard disk or RAM disk.

Media Master Plus also includes a CP/M emulation program for MS-DOS computers, which allows you to run CP/M software and use CP/M operating system commands from an MS-DOS computer.

Additional features of both utilities include an ability to select files with wildcard specifications and selective tagging, a "change diskette" prompt if you select more files than will fit on your diskette, and a choice of menu or command modes.

Other Software in this Category

CONVERT

Selfware, Inc.
3545 Chain Bridge Road, Suite 3
Fairfax, Virginia 22030
Telephone: (703) 352-2977
Sales: (800) 242-4355

CURSOR CONTROL UTILITIES

The cursor plays a very important role on the display screen—it is the communication mechanism between the computer and you. Cursor keys direct the cursor. The cursor orients you in your computer work, but a few other elements can interfere with this orientation.

The first interfering factor is the speed at which the keyboard transmits keystrokes to application software, which can vary for single and repeated keystrokes.

The second element is the keyboard type-ahead buffer, which defines the maximum number of keystrokes retained in memory if you type faster than the cursor can display. The buffer is used primarily to compensate for slowness in the other two elements. By this method, you may type faster than software can process keystrokes, and the software will read from the buffer when it is ready.

DOS automatically sets the size of the keyboard buffer to 15 characters. Some application software provides an additional type-ahead buffer, and some utilities allow you to specify buffer size.

The third factor is the speed at which your application software interprets and acts on keystrokes. If application software is slow compared to your typing speed and DOS's transmission speed, the buffer(s) will fill up, the keyboard will "beep," and no further keystrokes will be read until the software is ready.

An additional problem caused by a full buffer is that the screen does not display accurate information. For example, if you hold the space bar down for the equivalent of 20 spaces, the cursor may only move five spaces by the time you lift your finger. After you stop pressing the space bar, however, the cursor will "run on" for fifteen additional spaces.

Cursor control utilities are RAM-resident utilities that address one or more of these issues. The most common feature is speeding DOS response to the cursor and auto-repeat key entry. Many of these utilities allow you to adjust cursor speed, to select cursor speed when loading the utility, and to change cursor speed within the program.

Other features address repeating keystrokes separately from single-keystroke responsiveness. Another feature addresses run-on, which can be exacerbated by increased transmission speed or keyboard buffer size.

CRUISE CONTROL

Revolution Software, Inc.
715 Route 10 East
Randolph, New Jersey 07869
Telephone: (201) 366-4445

Software Features

Cruise Control offers three features that address cursor control. The first feature allows you to increase or decrease the speed of cursor and repeating keystrokes. Speed may be adjusted, even from within an application, while Cruise Control is resident.

The second, unique feature addresses cursor run-on. Cruise Control's "anti-skid breaking" adapts to the speed at which your application software can process keystrokes. Cursor and auto-repeating keys will stop when the key is released.

The third feature allows you to repeat any key or key combination without holding down the key. After you press a special key, the next keystroke is repeated until you stop it by pressing any key. Repeat speed may also be adjusted.

Because software response varies, Cruise Control offers four "strategies" that you may switch through until you find the optimal strategy for your software and preference. Cruise Control provides an extensive list of software programs and recommends a strategy for each.

Additional features included with Cruise Control are a time and date stamp macro (with a choice of formats) and an adjustable automatic screen blanker.

Other Software in this Category

ACCELERATOR:PC

SWFTE, Inc.
P.O. Box 219
Rockland, Delaware 19732
Telephone: (302) 658-1123

DISK CACHERS

Next to printing, disk access—reading from or writing to—is the most time-consuming computer operation. Loading programs and data files from disk is a relatively slow process. The disk access time required to process large data files while running a program can drastically reduce processing speed.

Hard disks can be accessed faster than floppy diskettes, which is one reason they are so popular. Hard disk drives still operate with some of the same mechanical functions as floppy drives, however, so they can still slow computer processing.

For this reason, many computer users set up RAM disks if computers are equipped with sufficient memory. RAM disks (or virtual disks) can electronically perform a disk's serving and receiving functions at a much greater speed.

RAM disks have neither the capacity nor the permanence of hard disks. At the beginning of a computer session, a RAM disk must be created and the desired programs and/or data files copied to it from disk storage. At the end of the operating session, new or revised data files must be written back to disk before the power is shut off, or they will be lost.

Disk **cachers** provide the best of both worlds. They are RAM-resident utilities that, in addition to using other management tactics, minimize disk access by using RAM as a buffer (or cache).

Generally, a disk cacher reads ahead on the disk for each read access and stores excess data in a buffer. In addition, data processed by application software remains in a buffer after the application releases it.

When an application requests data, the disk cacher searches buffers for the data before it resorts to a disk access. An application is likely to need the next segment of data or to reaccess previously processed data. In such situations, a trip to the disk is saved.

Disk information tends to fall into one of two extremes — data processed regularly but infrequently (e.g., the last record in your mailing list) and data accessed often (e.g., an application overlay file.) Obviously, applications that make use of the latter type of information stand to gain the most from disk cachers.

LIGHTNING

Personal Computer Support Group, Inc.
11035 Harry Hines Boulvard, Suite 207
Dallas, Texas 75229
Telephone: (214) 351-0564

Software Features

Lightning is a disk caching utility that employs efficient management techniques to minimize disk access.

Lightning chooses to maintain data in its buffers according to frequency of usage. Each time a sector of data is read, it is assigned to the top of the list, which is the first buffer to be searched and the last to be purged. Frequently accessed data can remain in the buffer throughout the operating session.

Lightning also minimizes disk writes by judging whether or not a disk write requested by application software is necessary. If data has not changed, Lightning skips the operation.

Other features that improve efficiency include purging buffers of data belonging to a subsequently removed diskette and refraining from intercepting data read from and written to a RAM disk. Disk access statistics can be displayed to inform you of improvements achieved by using Lightning.

Optional features include allocating specific amounts of RAM to Lightning buffers, turning caching on and off separately for each disk drive, and switching on and off a software write-protection feature for individual drives.

Other Software in this Category

FLASH

Software Masters Inc.
6352 North Guilford
Indianapolis, Indiana 46220
Telephone: (317) 253-8088

DCACHE

MicroWay, Inc.
PO Box 79
Kingston, Massachusetts 02364
Telephone: (617) 746-7341

INDEX

@Liberty, 199
1dir +, 50, 109

A

ACCELERATOR:PC, 311
ANSI.SYS, 131, 148, 152, 161
Archive, 31-32, 41, 43, 49, 51, 55, 59, 62
AUTOEXEC.BAT, 100, 131-132, 142, 151, 153
ASCII format, 18, 22, 34, 36, 45, 51, 56, 59, 62, 76, 99, 107, 109,
    112, 115, 117, 119, 120, 156, 161, 169, 170, 174, 176, 179, 187-188, 198,
    226, 228, 230, 233-234, 236, 237, 238, 245, 250, 255, 260-263, 267, 270,
    273, 275, 294, 307
ATTRIB, 32, 41
Attribute, 31, 49, 53, 55, 59, 61-62
AUTOEXEC.BAT, xiv, 254

B

Background communication, 129
Backup, xi, 9, 13, 15, 24-25, 28, 32, 41, 75, 104, 188-189, 192-193, 196,
    248, 270, 272, 277-299
BACKUP MASTER, 292
Backup utilities, 279
BACK-IT, 304
BAKUP, 304
BASIC, 141, 174, 230, 270-271, 276
Batch files, 47, 75, 77, 81, 85, 87, 89, 91, 99-101, 104, 106, 108, 109, 112,
    114, 122, 128, 147, 151, 170, 172, 174-175, 177, 181, 237, 254, 270, 274,
    284, 294
Bad sectors, 5-7, 9-10, 14, 17, 18, 20-21, 24-25, 27
Block operations, 51
Boot record, 5-9, 14
Bytes used, 48

C

C, 269
CARBON COPY PLUS, 251
CELL/MATE, 196
CHDIR (CD), 32
CHKDSK, 10-11, 14, 18, 38-39
Chronological file sort, 46
CLIPPER, 215
Clusters, 3, 6, 8, 10-11
COMMAND.COM, 5, 115, 133, 140

H

I

K

L

M

MACE+ UTILITIES, 23-25
Macintosh, 256
MACLINK PLUS, 256
Macro utility, xvii
Make utilities, 267
MEDIA MASTER, 308
Memory management, see RAM management
MEMORY/SHIFT, 149
Menu utilities, xii, 50, 54, 58, 66
MICROSOFT WINDOWS, 142
Miscellaneous utilities, 305
MKDIR (MD), 32, 36, 47
Modem, 86, 129, 251-254, 256, 307, 308
Monochrome monitor, ix
MORE, 37
Mouse, 58, 117, 136, 137, 142, 144, 147, 149
Move a file, 31, 34, 45-46, 52, 56, 60, 63
Multi-tasking utilities, x, xii, 66, 92, 124, 126, 129-135, 137-142, 146, 204,
    248-249, 254, 287, 292, 297, 300
MULTILINK ADVANCED, 253

N

Networking, 126, 244, 246, 248, 249, 250, 253, 254, 256
NEWKEY, 183
Non-continguous files, 14
NORTON COMMANDER, 54-57, 116
NORTON UTILITIES, 26-17, 54, 56
NOTE-IT, 197

O

On-screen clock, 58
One-finger typing, 165
Operating System, x, xi, xv, xvii, 17, 94, 133, 138-139, 142, 152, 156, 161,
    173, 245, 308
Orphaned data, 7, 10, 14, 18
Overlay files, xvi, 71, 72, 75, 110, 115, 117, 128, 170, 268

P

Q

R

RAM disks, xvi, 115, 134, 136, 140-141, 144, 146, 149, 308, 311-313

RAM management, xv, 79, 130, 133, 136, 140, 144, 146, 148, 150, 152, 176, 179, 182, 213

RAM-resident programs, xv, 20, 50, 54, 65, 79, 80, 83, 87, 90, 112, 115, 118, 128-129, 131-132, 143, 146, 148, 150, 152, 173, 197, 239, 240, 253, 270, 306, 310, 312

Read Only, 30-32, 41, 43-44, 49, 51, 55, 59, 62

RECOVER, 10, 14, 17, 25

Recover deleted files, 16

Recover removed subdirectories, 16

Redirection, 37

RELAY GOLD, 257

RELAY SILVER, 257

REMOTE, 257

Remote access, 246, 249, 251

Remove a directory, 35, 37, 47, 52, 57, 60, 63

Rename a directory, 35-36, 39, 47, 52, 57, 60, 63

RENAME, 50

REPORTS PLUS, 198

RESTORE, 32, 41

Restoring, 15

RE/CALL, 182

Redirect, 35

Reformat, 8, 12, 13

Re-organizing the path, 15

RMDIR (RD), 32, 36-37, 47

Root directory, 5-6, 8, 9, 14, 30

RS-232 cable, 253

Run program from within another, 71, 74, 78-79, 83, 87, 90, 118, 128-129, 143, 169, 170, 172, 178, 181, 235, 237, 240, 272, 302

R&R, 215

S

SAYWHAT?!, 276

SBT Database Accounting Library, 215

Screen design, 265

Screen saver, 54, 115, 172-173, 176, 178, 181

SCREEN SCULPTOR, 269

Search across directories, 33, 44, 51, 55, 59, 62

Search for specific text, 19, 27, 31, 33-34, 44, 51, 55, 59, 62

Sectors, 3, 19

SIDEKICK, 306

RELATED TITLES FROM MIS:PRESS